Kent Hrbek's
Tales from the
Minnesota
Twins Dugout

Kent Hrbek with Dennis Brackin

SportsPublishingLLC.com

ISBN-10: 1-59670-252-4
ISBN-13: 978-1-59670-252-3

Publishers: Peter L. Bannon and Joseph J. Bannon Sr.
Senior managing editor: Susan M. Moyer
Developmental editor: Erin Linden-Levy
Art director: K. Jeffrey Higgerson
Dust jacket design: Joseph Brumleve
Interior design: Kathryn R. Holleman

Sports Publishing L.L.C.
804 North Neil Street
Champaign, IL 61820
Phone: 1-877-424-2665
Fax: 217-363-2073
www.SportsPublishingLLC.com

Printed in the United States of America

CIP data available upon request.

DEDICATED TO THE MINNESOTA TWINS
AND THEIR GREAT FANS

Contents

CHAPTER ONE

The Twins Way

Whenever the Twins are successful, like they were in 2006, I hear people talking about "the Twins way." The Twins way is heavy on respect for the game, heavy on fundamentals, and heavy on fun.

I think what people are calling the Twins way started about the time Gary Gaetti, Tom Brunansky, and I walked into the Twins clubhouse for our first full year together in 1982. It had almost as much to do with cleaning fish in the clubhouse—until it got banned—as anything that happened on the field.

You could say we were a little different. One thing about my big-league career is that I did it the way I was taught—the old-fashioned way, some might call it.

Had a ton of fun. Didn't spend much time working out or watching what I ate. And I got out when I was 34 years old so I wouldn't miss my daughter's birthday parties and school plays, like I had watched so many of my teammates do.

Oh, did I mention I also have two World Series rings? That's the reason I played this game. Personal stats? Overrated.

Late in my career a writer told me a prominent executive from another American League club had once said, based on my physical frame and swing, I could have been one of the all-time greats. My numbers, he said, should have been Hall of Fame.

I think the writer thought I'd feel bad or something, like I hadn't lived up to my potential. I felt I lived up to my potential. Maybe I could have done things better. But who knows? My main goal was to win a World Series, and I was lucky enough to win two.

I think I was lying on the dugout bench at the time, watching some of my teammates stretch.

People will tell you I was never much for wind sprints or pregame stretching.

Homegrown

I look back at my career and wonder how lucky could one guy be? I grew up a couple miles from the old Metropolitan Stadium, a huge Twins fan. I played at Bloomington Kennedy High School, got drafted by the Twins, reached the majors with my hometown team at the age of 21 and played my whole career with one team.

Stop and think for a minute about how often that happens. How many kids get to play in the big leagues for their hometown team? And not only that, but hit a grand-slam home run in the World Series, and help their team win two Series titles. That just doesn't happen, especially in baseball today where guys jump teams as soon as they get a better offer. A lot of people have described me as a throwback, and I'm proud of that. Loyalty—to my team and my state—has always meant a lot to me. It just wouldn't have been the same to me playing in the big leagues for anybody but the Twins.

And today my wife, Jeanie, our daughter, Heidi, and I live in Bloomington, a couple miles from where I grew up. The ballpark where I played as a kid—Valley View—now has a four-field baseball complex that is named Kent Hrbek Fields. Can you believe that? That's cool as heck. I've got buddies I went to school with, and they'll tell me: "My kid is playing at Hrbek Fields this week." It feels pretty weird to hear them talking about a field named after me. I always thought they named fields after people who had died. And I'm not dead yet.

Growing Up Fast

But as much fun as it was, and as lucky as I was, it wasn't all a joyride. I was 21 years old, playing Class-A ball in Visalia, California, when I got the call. My mom told me that my dad had been to the doctor, and they thought he had Lou Gehrig's disease. I didn't even know what that was. All I knew was that Lou Gehrig had died from it.

I immediately told them I was coming home, and they said, "No, you're not. We're coming out there to see you." They didn't have the money to be flying around like that—my dad worked for the gas company, my mother had been a stay-at-home mom for me, my brother, and my sister—but they hopped on a plane and flew out to see me.

My dad didn't seem sick at all when they came out, so that made me feel a little better. But I soon learned how fast the disease progresses. Mom said she had noticed some slurred speech and he dragged his foot a little, but that happened mostly when he came back from his weekly bowling outing, and she thought maybe he had just had a few cocktails. But she kept noticing it, kept on him to go to the doctor, and that's how they found out.

I wanted to come home, but they wanted me to stay in California and play ball. My dad told me: "I got you here. I'm going to be at home, taking care of Mom. You keep going with what you're doing here."

Those were probably the best words my dad ever told me. When I look back, that conversation cleared my mind. From that point, my whole incentive was to get back home and get called up by the Twins.

Heading Home

I had a great year at Visalia, batting .379 with 27 homers and 111 RBIs in 121 games. I walked into the clubhouse on August 22, and five or six of the guys were already there.

They said Skip—Dick Phillips—wanted to talk to me. I went in thinking, "Geez, I'm getting called up to AA." I remember the first thing Phillips said to me was, "Hrbie, the Twins are playing in New York Monday night, and Billy Gardner wants you to play first." I just stood there. No response. I couldn't believe it. Finally, the first thing I said was, "How do I get there?"

I was fired up, because I knew I was going home.

The Debut

On Monday night, I was in the lineup, playing first base at Yankee Stadium where Lou Gehrig once played. I look back now and that seems pretty ironic. A few months earlier I had learned my dad was dying of Lou Gehrig's disease, and my first taste of the big leagues was standing on the same piece of ground where Lou Gehrig played. I hit a home run in the 12th inning to win that game. Exciting? I was up all night calling everyone back home.

A few days later my dad got to see me play in the big leagues. That meant a lot to me. But the next year, in 1982 during my rookie season, he died. And that's one of the reasons I retired early.

I'm not saying we were a huggy-kissy family growing up. But we were a family—my mom and dad, brother Kevin and younger sister Kerry. We ate dinners together, my parents came to 90 percent of my ballgames, and they were there for me whenever I needed them.

And I respected them, which is what families have to have. I remember swearing one time as a kid and my brother said he was going to tell Mom, because she'd wash my mouth out with soap.

Well, I ran to beat my brother home, and I went in the bathroom and stuck a bar of soap in my mouth so Mom wouldn't have the pleasure of doing it.

Maybe some people don't understand why I walked away from the big leagues so young. But when I turned 34, my daughter turned two. I decided I was going to watch her grow up, and be a dad. I wasn't going to miss all those years.

Besides, by that point, I'd already had a heckuva run.

CHAPTER TWO

Shadows of the Met

No. 6: Tony-O

My earliest memory of playing on a team was right here in Bloomington, playing T-ball when I was about six years old. We didn't have uniforms or anything, but the coach told us that we should all wear white T-shirts so we looked like a team. Or at least look the same when everybody is heading the wrong way on the base paths, which is what T-ball is all about.

But there was something about swinging a bat at a ball that I loved right away. Plus, I loved my first uniform, such as it was. My mom sewed the No. 6 on my back—not an iron-on number, but actually hand stitched—because even then I was a big Tony Oliva fan. Tony could flat-out hit, and he was left-handed like I was. At age six, that was plenty of reason to idolize a guy.

I lived close enough to the old Met as a kid to ride my bike to the ballpark. Monday nights were discounted for seniors and under 16s, and we used to go to a lot of Monday night games. My dad would take me to some games, and other times I'd go with friends. I loved the outfield stands at the old Met. There was a lot of entertainment going on besides the game itself. We'd play tag under the bleachers some nights. Other times we'd get the seats over the bullpen and talk to relievers. I wish I knew then what I know now, because my teammate, Ron Davis, would trade baseballs for bratwurst as he sat in the bullpen. I'd have had a lot more baseballs, and eaten a lot fewer brats, as a kid.

When I did watch the games, the guy I watched was Tony-O. I can still recite his stats: first player to win the batting title in his first two seasons, three batting titles in all. He was among the top three in batting seven times in eight seasons, starting with his rookie year in 1964. When I got to the big leagues people assumed that Harmon Killebrew must have been my favorite player as a kid. But I always focused on watching Tony swing the bat and hit the ball to all fields. Believe me, I loved it when Harmon hit those tape-measure homers. But for some reason, I liked the way Tony slapped the ball around better than home runs.

I think that surprised a lot of people, because I was a big guy playing first base, and people just naturally thought I should be a home-run hitter. Now, I've got nothing against home runs. But I always hated striking out, and that's the price you pay if you're trying to hit homers all the time. I always had the attitude that nothing gets accomplished when you strike out. But if you put the ball in play someplace, something can happen. I always prided myself on on-base percentage more than home runs. My career on-base percentage was .367, which is pretty good for a guy who batted cleanup most of his career. I'm also proud that I had more walks (838) than strikeouts (798). I think even Tony-O would have been proud of those numbers.

Learning the Game

The most important thing as far as developing my game wasn't organized youth baseball. I mean, those games were fun, getting to wear a uniform and playing in front of your mom and dad. But where I learned the game was playing wiffle ball in the

In Bloomington Little League, I was the tallest kid on my team (middle row, third from right). Courtesy of Kent Hrbek

neighborhood backyards. We always had a ballgame going, and we had holes worn in the yard where first, second, and third base were. Every time I think about that, I remember Harmon telling me that when his dad would get upset because the kids were ruining the yard, his mom would yell, "Hey, what are we raising here, kids or grass?" That's the same attitude my parents had.

My buddies on the block—the Meyers brothers: Jimmy, Russ, and Monte—had the perfect place for a baseball field in their backyard. The Meyers' backyard is probably where I learned the game best—how to hit different pitches because of all the things they were able to make that damned wiffle ball do. I learned to hit curveballs, knuckleballs, you name it. I can't tell you how many times we stood in the backyard and played until it was so dark we couldn't see anymore. We always tried to emulate Twins players, from the top of the order to the bottom, guys like Cesar Tovar and Rod Carew. We had their batting stances down. And if you were Dean Chance, you had to strike out to make it real life. Poor Dean couldn't hit, but he sure could pitch.

I've always been someone who just loved playing games. You name the game; I love it. And I love to win. I used to play Candyland with my daughter, and I admit I tried to beat her. I suppose that's not real nice, but that's just the way I am. I'm not even sure where that came from—my dad, for sure, and probably my high school baseball coach, Buster Radebach, who used to play in the Boston Red Sox system.

But it has to be fun, too; otherwise I'm not going to do it. I'm a big guy, and people figured I must have been a good high school football player. Well, the last time I played football was seventh grade. I hated the idea of practice, practice, practice, practice four days a week, then play one game. Four days of work for one day of fun.

Baseball was different. Even the practices were fun. You'd get to step in the batting cage and hit, or take fielding practice. There's something about baseball that felt like a game every time you stepped onto the field. Not like football.

Now, I played a lot of other sports at the park. I was good in everything, even hockey…except for basketball. The one thing I could never do was dribble a basketball. So by the time I got to high school, I wasn't playing football or basketball. Nope, the only sport I played was baseball.

Switching Positions

I wasn't a superstar in junior high. There were always a couple guys on the team who had better stats than I did. I had always been a shortstop and pitcher in youth baseball. The summer before I went to Kennedy High, there was a guy on the team named Marty Petersen, who was a shortstop and a sophomore. I was a ninth grader. They needed a first baseman on the summer team, and I said, "Hey, I'll give it a shot."

Our coach, Phil Smith, stuck me over there at first, hit me a ton of ground balls, and I survived. I never played shortstop again. I guess I should say thanks to Phil Smith and Marty Petersen for making me a first baseman.

We made the high school state tournament my sophomore year at Bloomington Kennedy, and Timmy Laudner's Park Center team beat us in the first round 4-1. I remember I dunked a little double over the third baseman's head. But another thing I remember is that Timmy played center field, believe it or not. I didn't even know him at the time, but he would become a teammate and good friend of mine with the Twins. The guy I remember more than Tim from that game was a pitcher named Donnie Nolan, who threw harder than anybody I'd ever seen.

But maybe the most important thing to happen to me that year was a game we played at Wayzata during the regular season. Wayzata had a big stud catcher named Dave Vanzo. The Chicago Cubs had a scout in the stands that day watching him play, and I hit two home runs, which was pretty good for a skinny sophomore. As I'm walking to the bus, the scout grabbed my arm and said, "Mr. Hrbek."

That was the first time anyone ever called me "Mr. Hrbek." He told me he saw the way I played the game, and wondered whether I had any interest in playing baseball beyond high school. That was kind of a jolt, because as a sophomore I wasn't the kind of kid who thought too far out. I got on the bus and wondered, "What was that guy talking to me about? Do I have an opportunity to play this game?" From that day on, there were scouts at most of my games. I guess word spreads pretty fast in the scouting fraternity.

After my junior year, I went to a couple of tryout camps just to see how I'd fit in. I remember going to a Cincinnati camp, and a Dodger camp. What I learned is that I didn't run fast enough for those two organizations.

I could hit the ball off the wall all day long, but I couldn't run. At least not fast enough for those guys. Now, I was pretty fast. In fact, my rookie year with the Twins in 1982, I was the fastest guy on the team, which probably said more about that team than it did about me. We lost 102 games that year and stole 38 bases. That's the team total, not mine.

If you remember Cincinnati and Los Angeles in the '70s, they were both built around speed and stolen bases. So they'd take stopwatches out and time you sprinting. I always wondered why they didn't pay more attention to me hitting balls off the wall. But I guess they were too busy timing the wind sprints.

Twins Enter the Picture

Smokey Teewalt is the guy who got the Twins interested in me. Smokey was a concession guy at the old Met Stadium, and his son was the same age as me. I played against him when he was at Bloomington Lincoln, which was only a couple miles from my school, Kennedy. I've heard that it was the summer of my sophomore year that he went and told George Brophy, the chief scout for the Twins, that someone should go and check this Hrbek kid out.

So they sent Angelo Guiliani, the Twins area scout, to watch me. I saw Angelo around the ball parks a lot my junior and senior years, and the summer after my senior year at Kennedy the Twins drafted me in the 17th round, fairly late, partly because I had already signed a letter of intent to play college ball at the University of Minnesota.

The first offer the Twins made was for $5,000. I turned that down, although not because I had my heart set on going to college. When it came to school, I wasn't a guy who skipped classes and stuff, mostly because I was afraid Mom and Dad would whoop my ass. But I admit I wasn't the brightest bulb on the tree.

George Thomas was coaching the Gophers at the time and after my senior year in high school I played on his summer league team. He told me if I could get the money I wanted, I should sign and go straight to professional baseball. That's a little weird for a college coach to say that to a kid, but he was fired up about the way I could play the game. I love George Thomas for being honest with me. He saw I had a better future on the ball field than the classroom. Plus, he was one of the funniest guys I know.

My dad pretty much left it up to me. We talked about signing, and we decided that if I could get $30,000 I'd sign. We figured that would cover my schooling if I didn't make it in pro ball, although the truth is I was about as big on the thought of going to school as I was on jumping into a pot of boiling water.

It didn't seem to matter much, because the Twins didn't look too anxious to fork over that kind of bonus for a 17th-round draft choice. As baseball fans know, Calvin Griffith, the Twins owner, wasn't known for handing out money.

But Angelo kept watching me after the draft. Finally, one night he got Brophy and Calvin to come to a game at Valley View, which was across the street from my house. I remember that night mostly because there was a hush over the ballpark; everyone knew Calvin and Brophy were there to watch Hrbek. I hit a long home run to right-center field, but I don't even know if Calvin and Brophy stayed the entire game. We never talked after the game or anything, so I had no idea whether they were impressed or not. As the summer went on, it began to look more and more like I was going to college.

At the end of the summer our Legion team made the state playoffs and went to Austin, Minnesota, to play at McCracken Field. That's a park where former Yankees star Moose Skowron supposedly hit the longest home run ever hit there. Well, I hit one straight over the center-field fence that the old timers said was longer than the one Skowron hit.

We ended up getting beat by Terry Steinbach's team from New Ulm, but as we were heading to the bus, Angelo stopped me at the door and said, "I think I can get you the money, kid." I guess that's the story of my life as an amateur player—getting stopped by scouts as I was about to get on the bus.

I ended up signing right after that, although it was too late in the summer to send me to rookie ball. They told me to report to Instructional League in the fall. I have to admit I wasn't quite honest with my dad about using that money for school if pro ball didn't pan out. I took a good chunk of that $30,000 and bought myself a Ford pickup. In my mind, I was done with school. If this baseball thing didn't pan out, I figured I'd rather pump gas at the neighborhood filling station.

This was at my high school graduation party in 1978. Hard to believe that four months later I started my pro career in the Instructional League. Courtesy of Kent Hrbek

CHAPTER THREE

My First Love

My dislike of practices wasn't the only reason I gave up football at an early age. Football is played in the fall. To me the fall is for hunting, not throwing around a pigskin and smashing into bodies.

A lot of people aren't going to believe me when I say this, but the outdoors—and by that I mean fishing and hunting—is definitely my first love. Don't get me wrong, I loved playing baseball, and almost all sports, except for trying to dribble that damn basketball. But I get just as jacked up going fishing with a bunch of guys in Canada on a five-day trip as I got jacked up to play in the World Series.

I'd lose sleep over going on a fishing trip with my buddies. That didn't happen too often playing baseball, except for the nights Gary Gaetti and I sipped cocktails all night. I just love packing the cooler and sitting around a campfire with the guys, and getting up early the next morning to go fishing. There's nothing like it.

We went to the White House after winning the World Series in 1987, and I couldn't wait to get back to Minnesota. We literally got off the plane and climbed in a motor home that was waiting in my driveway to take a pheasant-hunting trip to South Dakota. Now that's living.

Summers at Grandpa's

I think my love of the outdoors came from my dad and my grandpa, Pete Kiminski, my mom's dad. To this day I idolize my grandpa, because he could basically live off the land.

He lived up in the Willow River area about 40 miles south of Duluth, an hour and a half north of the Twin Cities. You hit that area and it's like you're in the North Woods. I used to go up for the summer and chase frogs and catch minnows out of the creek that we'd use for fishing.

My grandpa was the guy who always organized the hunts every fall, telling the other guys, "You go here, you go there." You didn't hunt with him unless you listened to him. And kids didn't hunt with his group, period. He died in 1973 when I was 13, right about the time that he would have allowed me to start hunting.

But even though I didn't get to hunt with him, he's probably where I got most of my love for the outdoors. My dad was a big part of that, too.

My mom and dad used to rent a cabin every August outside of Brainerd and spend a week there fishing. My memories of my dad are more from those weeks at the cabin than hitting grounders to me in the backyard, or any baseball game. I used to look forward to that week all year. Want to know where I learned about loyalty and commitment? My baseball team in the Bloomington Athletic Association qualified for the playoffs one year and it was the exact same week we had reserved the Brainerd cabin. My dad drove me down in the afternoon for the games, and then we'd turn around and go back right after. I think too many people take the easy way out in those situations and put their vacation first. My dad wasn't that way, and it always stuck with me.

I was about 16 when I got to go on my first deer hunt with my dad. We were hunting on my uncle's land, up in the same area where my grandparents lived. I went out with my dad early in the morning, and he put me up next to a tree and told me to sit there. I always like to use my ears as much as my eyes and listen for sounds, because most of the time in the woods you hear stuff before you can see it.

Well, I heard this crunch, crunch, crunch of something coming up through the leaves, I looked and there was a little squirrel running around. Pretty soon I heard a crunch, crunch, crunch again. I figured it was that squirrel, but I turned around and looked, and there was this little eight-point buck. I shot, and he went down on the first shot. True story. I got a deer on my first shot.

I was so fired up. My dad came running over when he heard the shot, yelling, "Way to go! Way to go!" Then he got out his knife and started gutting the deer. It was perfect, because I not only shot a deer, but I didn't have to gut him. My dad was known as the gutter. Whenever someone shot something, he was there with his knife, ready to gut. As you might guess, he was pretty well liked by everyone he hunted with.

Not Always Compatible

My love of the outdoors didn't always mix well with baseball, which I learned about, oh, a week into my professional career. After I signed with the Twins and reported to the fall Instructional League in Florida, I immediately bought a fishing rod and headed to the ocean shore to try my hand at saltwater fishing. Johnny Castino also liked to fish, and was my guide on that first trip, although I'm sure Johnny doesn't want to take credit for it.

We were casting off a jetty, and I wanted to get as far out on the rocks as I could. I walked out along the rocks and slipped, falling into some coral, which is like sliding your leg along razor

Hunting and fishing were my first loves and I often shared them with my teammates. Tim Laudner (left), Steve Lombardozzi (second from left), and Gary Gaetti (second from right) joined me on this pheasant hunt. Courtesy of Kent Hrbek

blades. I didn't even know I was hurt, but I looked down and there was blood all over the water, and my ankle was slit. I still have the scar.

I ended up at the doctor's office getting my ankle stitched. When the doctor finished, he said it took 13 stitches to close the cut. I told him that 13 wasn't a very good number, and asked him if he could add another one. He was nice about it, and put one more in so I could have 14, which is a good number for me since it became my uniform number with the Twins.

At the time, there was nothing lucky about the number, or the fishing trip, for me. It happened at exactly the same time Twins manager Gene Mauch arrived in Melbourne to watch a week of Instructional League games. Oh, did he chew my ass out. He told me, "I come down here to watch you play, and you guys are out farting around fishing, and you cut your ankle all to hell."

Then he pointed over at Castino, and said, "You see that guy there? He just doesn't do a lot of things right, and I'm not sure he's ever going to make it."

The next year Castino was playing for Mauch in the big leagues, and he was co-American League Rookie of the Year with Alfredo Griffin. I knew Gene Mauch was a great manager and all that. But when I got to the big leagues and we played California when he was managing the Angels, I wanted to kick his butt because he told me Johnny Castino wasn't a very good ballplayer. I always thought Cas was one of the toughest competitors I ever played with—a guy who hated the opposition and would do whatever it took to win.

The Lure of Fishing

When I got called up to the big leagues late in the 1981 season I lived at home in Bloomington. Pretty convenient, to be playing in the majors and living with Mom and Dad. There probably aren't too many guys who can say that. In 1982 and '83, Tom Brunansky and I rented a little house in Richfield. We called it the ODC—the on-deck circle. There were plenty of parties, with Domino's pizza and beer as the nightly special.

Before the '84 season, I bought a place on Lake Minnetonka, and took in Brunansky as a roommate. Bruno liked to fish a bit, too, and there were a few charter flights back after road trips where we'd land at 5 a.m., drive home from the airport and as the sun was coming up jump into the boat to do a little early morning fishing.

Over the years, I had quite a few teammates who liked to fish. Dave Engle, who became Bruno's brother-in-law when they married sisters, lived on Lake Minnetonka, too, although Engle was more of a lake cruiser than a fisherman. Kirby Puckett liked

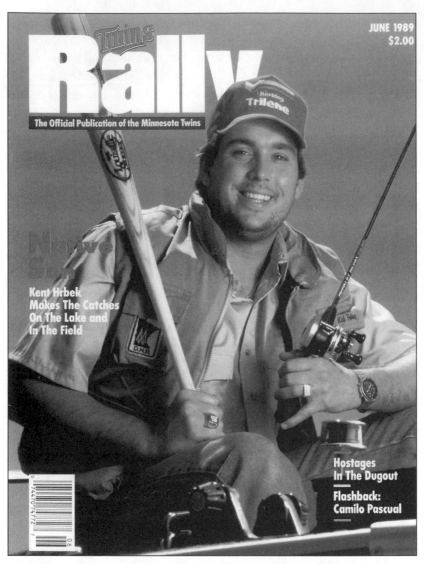

TWINS

Rally

The Official Publication of the Minnesota Twins

JUNE 1989
$2.00

Kent Hrbek
Makes The Catches
On The Lake and
In The Field

Hostages
In The Dugout

Flashback:
Camilo Pascual

The Twins put me on the cover of their fan magazine, highlighting my love of fishing. I think I did a good job of balancing work and play.

Courtesy of the Minnesota Twins

to fish, and the thing about Puck is that any fish that landed in his boat ended up in his live well, destined for his dinner plate. Puck was one of those guys who kept every fish he caught.

Fishing was always my getaway, and not just at home. Dick Martin, our trainer, was an avid fisherman, and when we found we had that in common we used to take fishing trips on the road. We'd fish for trout in Cleveland, go salmon fishing when we were in Seattle and head to a reservoir in Texas. There were other cities where I'd ask the clubhouse kids where the fish were biting, and we'd get up early in the morning and head out there.

When we were in Milwaukee, I used to take charter boats out on Lake Michigan. One time the guy who owned our minor-league club in Kenosha took Rick Aguilera and me out fishing. It was horrible, windy weather, and Aggie got sicker than a dog. He puked the whole time, which wasn't too good because we had a game that night.

When we got to the ballpark that afternoon, Aggie came up and said, "Hrbie, make sure we win by a bunch, so I don't have to pitch." We ended up winning by a few runs, and he came up to me after the game and said thanks.

That was a lot to go through for one brown trout, which was all we caught that day.

That little outing on Lake Michigan was the exception. I usually used common sense and knew that I couldn't go on an all-day outing because I'd be all pooped out and tired. Not that I didn't bend the rule once in a while.

RD's Mistake

I can't say Ron Davis always displayed common sense when it came to fishing. Next to me, RD might have been the most avid fisherman to play for the Twins during my years with the club.

RD was a different cat. Nicest guy in the world, but he went about things a little differently. He was our closer in the mid-

'80s—or at least he tried to be our closer—and there were games he'd give up four home runs in the ninth inning and afterward be singing "Jimmy Crack Corn" in the clubhouse. A lot of guys didn't care too much for that, although I knew he was just blowing off steam. A couple times RD broke down and cried after blowing a lead, which he did fairly frequently in the mid-'80s. There were a lot of us who were crying right along with him.

But I always liked RD, because I knew he cared, and he was always trying to do his best. And how can you not like a guy who shows up with a cooler full of bass just before a ballgame?

RD had this place up by Chisago Lakes, about 45 minutes north of Minneapolis, that he used to fish all the time. The bass must have been hitting real good, because one afternoon RD came running into the clubhouse with that cooler full of bass. He had stayed too long fishing, and didn't have time to swing by his house.

So he headed straight to the trainer's room and dumped his mess of flopping bass into the sink, and proceeded to clean them. We had guys in the whirlpool a couple feet away, getting ready for the game, and RD was cleaning his fish in the sink.

Ray Miller, our manager at the time, found out about it and banned fish in the clubhouse. I guess that was OK, but Ray was so fired up he told us he didn't want us out in the sun, which meant he didn't want us fishing during the day. Well, that lasted about two hours with me, although Ray probably had some basis for his edicts.

I know one time I had been fishing at Mille Lacs and I got so sunburned that when I got to the ballpark I could barely put on my uniform. That memory was probably on Ray's mind when he banned outdoor activities.

Still, Ray didn't crack my list of favorite managers. He was a nice, sincere guy, but I didn't know if he was ever going to make a great manager—a great pitching coach, but not much of a manager, at least with us. Then again, he had RD as his closer.

Meeting Jeanie

It was hunting, not baseball, that allowed me to meet my wife, Jeanie. I was deer hunting up by my grandparents' home in the fall of '81, after my first taste of the big leagues. We heard that a guy had shot a nice deer in a hunting camp by us. I said to the buddy I was hunting with—he was actually the brother of the girl I was dating at the time—that we should head over to that camp and see what the guy shot.

When we got there, the guy had a nice deer. We started talking to him and found out he was from Bloomington and lived about 10 blocks away from where I grew up. He said he was going to take the deer to a meat shop and weigh it when he got home, and I told him I'd be glad to help him out.

As fate would have it, the guy did call me for help when he got home, and my buddy and I went over to his house. We took the deer to the shop, weighed it, and went back to his house to have a beer and talk hunting in his basement. That's when Jeanie walked down the stairs. If she hadn't been home that night, I'd have never met her. I told my buddy on the way out to the car that the guy really had a nice-looking daughter, which maybe wasn't the best thing to say since I was dating his sister. But there was something special about Jeanie, and I saw it immediately.

But it took me a year to ask her out. I'd stop by to visit with her dad, Gene Burns, and have a beer and talk hunting. I liked Gene, because we shared similar interests. But I did have some ulterior motives for visiting him. The problem was, it was pretty apparent Jeanie wasn't quite as taken with me as I was with her. The truth is she had no interest in having anything to do with me. But I kept visiting Gene, and finally got her to go out with me.

I finally won her over, and we were married in 1985. I give her a lot of credit for keeping me on the straight and narrow. I could have been a pretty wild guy living in this town and playing ball. I loved to party and I loved to have a good time. But she

I met my wife Jeanie thanks to my love of the outdoors. Here is an indoor shot from a Twins Family Day gathering at the Dome.
Courtesy of the Minnesota Twins

knew when to tighten the reins when I needed that. Honestly, if it wasn't for her, I don't think I'd have had the career I did.

There is another benefit to our relationship: I still hunt with Geno every year. And he's become a father to me. After my dad died, Gene became the guy who showed me how to fix things around the house. Plumbing problem? I call Gene. I'm a pretty lucky guy to have been on that hunting trip in the fall of '81.

Maybe that's why hunting and fishing are my first loves.

CHAPTER FOUR

Headed to the Pros

Calling Home

For all the Grizzly Adams toughness I might portray as an outdoors guy, I wasn't quite that tough when I signed my first pro contract and reported to the Instructional League in Melbourne in the fall of 1978. We had a phone booth outside the back of the place we stayed. The booth looked like something straight out of an old movie, with a light that came on when you shut the door.

My first week in Florida I'm surprised I didn't single-handedly burn the light bulb out. There were some four-hour phone calls back home to my mom and my girlfriend. I cried on the phone a bunch of times, calling home and asking: "What am I doing? Is this what I want to do with my life?"

No way was I prepared to start a career. Heck, the flight to Florida for Instructional League was the first time I'd ever been on a plane. I suppose it's a lot like kids leaving for college their freshman year. You've got to get to know some people, and take your mind off of home.

No matter where I played, I never forgot how much I wanted to get back home. I always had this thing stuck in the back of my mind: Boy, if I can make it to the big leagues, I'm going home. Who knows, if I had been drafted by another organization, maybe I'd never even have made it to the big leagues because I wouldn't have had that same drive to get there.

Even though I was homesick that fall, I did love going to the ballpark. It didn't take me long to realize that as jobs go, it wasn't too bad to go to the ballpark in the morning, and be done in time to head to the ocean for fishing in the afternoon. And eventually I learned how to wash my own clothes, and feed myself, which has always been pretty important to me.

The two guys who probably pulled me through and helped me understand the game more than anybody right away were Gary Ward and my fishing buddy Johnny Castino.

Gary was a father figure for me. I think that's probably why they had me room with him. It's funny looking back. Gary was a black guy, and I had never spent any time with black folks. Not that that's good or bad. It's just a fact. There just weren't many blacks in Bloomington back then. I think we had one black student at Kennedy High School.

But at the time, Gary was a seasoned minor-league veteran. He later came up and had a couple good years with the Twins. Back then, he told me how to do this and that, and how to get ready for a game.

Johnny was more a peer, and I idolized him for the way he played the game. Despite the little fishing mishap off the jetty, I got through Instructional League. I don't think anyone would have predicted they'd be naming baseball fields after me in Bloomington, but I made it.

On to the Minors

Next stop was my first minor-league spring training camp in Melbourne. That's where I first met Tom Kelly, also known as

TK, who would become my manager with the Twins. Our first meeting is something we'd both like to forget.

We were playing a scrimmage game after workouts, and I swung and fouled a ball off the third-base line. My cleats stuck in the dirt, and my leg didn't turn on my follow-through. I felt something pop in my knee, and I fell down in the batter's box. TK came running over to the field and I grabbed his ankle because I was in terrible pain.

It turned out that my kneecap was dislocated. I hadn't even played in a game yet, and they sent me back home to rehabilitate it. Nice start to my pro career.

If you're keeping score, I'd pissed off the big-league manager, Gene Mauch, by slicing up my ankle fishing in the Instructional League, and blown out my knee before the first game in spring training. I'm guessing Calvin Griffith was wondering whether he could get his $30,000 back about then.

I spent about three months at home rehabilitating my knee, and in late June I headed to Elizabethton to play in half-season rookie league ball. I lasted 17 games before suffering the same injury. Once again, I was at the plate. I swung, and hit a ball into the right-center field gap. But my knee popped, and I hit the dirt instead of heading to first base. My teammate, Brad Carlson, was on second, and I knocked him in. He touched home, stopped, looked down at me and said, "Yo, Hrbie, what the hell's wrong with you?" I'm guessing Brad didn't end up in medical school after his pro career ended.

Check out my stats in those 17 games: .203 batting average, one home run and 15 strikeouts. Great first impression.

This time they sent me home and I had surgery on the knee to tighten the muscles around the kneecap and keep it from popping in and out. At that point I was not as worried about my paltry numbers at Elizabethton as I was about getting my knee back together.

I never had any knee problems during my high school career. After the surgery, the Twins' doctors and I talked about what

Here I am in my first minor-league uniform when I played for Rookie League Elizabethton in 1979. Nice curls, huh?
Courtesy of the Minnesota Twins

might have been causing the problem. We decided that I should try wearing rubber cleats, and not steel spikes like everyone else. The thinking was that the steel cleats were getting caught in the dirt and somehow preventing my knees from turning on my swing. So the rest of my career I wore rubber cleats, kind of like a soccer shoe. Maybe it did have something to do with the steel cleats, because it never happened again.

But from that point on my knees ached, along with most of the rest of my body. My whole career it seems like something always ached—ankles, shoulders, knees, everything hurt. I had wrist problems from jamming my hands when I slid. If it wasn't one thing, it was another. I learned to deal with it as part of the job.

Overall, though, things took a turn for the better after the second surgery. I went back to spring training in 1980 at Melbourne, started doing pretty well, and got sent to the Wisconsin Rapids, a Class-A farm club. I thought that was a great deal, because it was less than four hours from home, and also had a bunch of good fishing lakes. At that point I was thinking that life is pretty good. I soon learned otherwise.

Tough Love

Enter Rick Stelmaszek, Wisconsin Rapids manager. Stelly was barely older than we were, but he was the toughest, roughest kid I ever met in my life up until then. He was a south Chicago guy from the baddest part of town—I think they made that song up about him. I wasn't too fond of him back then, which is putting it mildly.

Now, I look back and realize that Stelly was just trying to make me a better player, even if I couldn't see that at the time. Stelly wasn't a guy who spent a lot of time worrying about whether his players liked him.

I remember there were a couple games we had a tough time fielding the ball in the infield, which isn't surprising in minor-league parks because the balls take some weird bounces. Well, Stelly had a plan to get us more familiar with those bounces. He had all the infielders go to our positions, lie down on our stomachs and he hit us grounders so we could watch the way the ball bounced. Now I'm not talking average grounders. He hit rockets at our heads and we had to put our gloves up in front of our faces to protect ourselves.

My birthday is May 21, near the start of the season for us. I had a little birthday party and ended up falling on my face, busting up my chin and forehead, and cutting my lip. It happens when you're 20. I still have a scar on top of my lip from that one. You can probably tell I'd had a little too much to drink at my own party. So the next day when I got to the ballpark, I went in to see Stelly and said, "Hey, I'm in pretty rough shape today." Stelly looked up at my face, with all those cuts and bruises, saw my bloodshot eyes and said: "You're in there for nine of the finest, kid." True to his word, Stelly made sure I played the entire game.

Of course, Stelly went on to be the longest tenured coach in Twins history. He was at 26 years in the big leagues in 2006. I had him as a coach with the Twins my whole career. And I'll tell you something: He's a puppy now compared to what he was like back then. As I said, I didn't like the guy much when he was my manager. I love him now, because I look back and say, "This guy taught me a helluva lot about baseball." I think that's why he's been around as long as he has. I'm sure there are a lot of scientists or mathematicians who hated their high school science and math teachers, but look back and say they're the reason for where they are today. I feel like that about Stelly.

The Trip

My career got on track that summer with the Wisconsin Rapids. I batted .267 with 19 homers and 76 RBIs in 115 games, and walked more (61) than I struck out (54). I played in the all-star game, and I think my home-run total was up there with anyone in the league.

It was also the summer I became friends with Gary Gaetti, who, as the years went on, became my closest friend in baseball. I met G-Man at Elizabethton the year before, but I wasn't around long enough to get to know him too well. Besides, Gary was already married, and when you're there for as short a time as I was you don't really get a chance to know the married guys.

In the spring of 1980 we were both sent to the Wisconsin Rapids. I got there early to find a place to stay. The day of our first game, we were all wondering, "Where's G-Man?" Well, he drove from Melbourne with his wife, and on the day of the game he pulled into the parking lot. He had this old pickup, his wife, Debby, sitting next to him and all their belongings in the back covered by an old sheet that was flapping away in the wind. Gary, as he usually did, looked all scruffy, because he's a guy who can grow a full beard in about half an hour. I watched that truck drive into the lot and I was thinking, "These people look like the Clampetts." Welcome to the minor leagues.

The next spring, I climbed in my Ford pickup truck—paid for with the money I got from the Twins because no way was I going back to school—and headed to Melbourne for spring training. I was figuring I would make the AA team at Orlando— seemed logical to go from Class A Wisconsin Rapids to AA after a good year—and it was going to be great because I would have my pickup truck with me in Florida for the whole summer. Plus I knew G-Man was going to be on that team, along with Tim Laudner, my old high school rival.

It was all perfect, except for the fact that TK, the manager at Orlando, came up to me two days before the other Class A team, Visalia, was supposed to break camp. TK told me, "Hrbie we've got some bad news. We're going to keep Shane Hallberg to play first base at AA, because he's older and has been around longer."

So there I was in Melbourne, Florida, with a four-wheel-drive pickup, and I've got to be in Visalia, California, in three days to meet the team. What are you going to do? I jumped in and started driving.

Fortunately, Scotty Madison, a catcher who later spent some time in the big leagues with the Tigers, decided to ride along with me. That was a big advantage, since I was still pretty green when it came to traveling. Heck, I'd never even seen most of the country that we were about to drive through.

Scotty went to Vanderbilt University, and I'm told he could have been the mayor of Nashville because he knew everybody in the whole county, and a whole lot of other places as well. The first night, we stayed in Tallahassee, where he was from originally. Then we drove until we were halfway across Texas and slept on the side of the road because Scotty didn't know anybody in the middle of Texas, which was a little surprising. The next night we stayed with the dean of Arizona State University, who was a friend of Scotty's family, and we got up the next morning and made it the rest of the way.

The next day we opened the season in Visalia. When you're young, you don't even think about being tired. Now I'd be thinking, "What the hell did I do that for? I'm beat." Back then, it just seemed like one more adventure. But looking back, I'm awful glad I had Scotty with me.

California Dream Season

We had an awesome team at Visalia. We had four guys with 100 RBIs, and were running away with the league title. Guys like Scotty Madison, Jim Weaver (who they called Dream Weaver), Jimmy Christensen, a pitcher named Paul Voigt, and I had great seasons. And Dick Phillips was a veteran manager who let us go out and play. After a year of Stelly, that was a welcome change.

But there were some tough times off the field, and not just because it was the summer I learned my dad had ALS. I think I was making maybe $500 a month, and I had to wire home for money a couple times. I was living with a kid named Kevin Williams, and we lived off fried egg sandwiches, because bread and eggs were about as cheap as you could go. One day I came home from the grocery with a dozen eggs and dropped them on the kitchen floor. I almost started crying. There was my dinner for the next week, and I had no money.

We learned to make do. That included beer, which by then had become a favorite beverage of mine. One night we pulled into the stadium at Reno early for batting practice, and there were several full beer kegs sitting outside the door of the stadium, waiting for the concession crew. My buddy, Rick Austin, who we called Woofie, was a catcher on the team. We saw the beer kegs, and told Woofie to empty out his catcher's bag, put a keg in and hide it in the back of the bus. We got back to Visalia that night and had a nice party. The beer was a little foamy from the bumpy ride back, but we made do.

Woofie was the kind of character you met in the minors. We lived together for the short time I was in Elizabethton, then roomed together the next year at Wisconsin Rapids. Stelly gave him the name Woofie. Rick had one speed, and that was forward. He was a stocky, short-fingered, muscular guy. He had a cup of coffee in the Twins major-league spring training camp one year because we needed extra catchers with all the pitchers throwing.

I spent a lot of time with him those first three years, and when he didn't make it to the majors, it was tough. It's a funny thing looking back at those days in the minors. You'd see some guys you thought were awesome, and they never made it to the bigs. You'd see other guys who you didn't think had a shot, and they ended up having long careers.

When the writing was on the wall for Woofie, I think he had a pretty good head about it. Life went on. You learned that in the minors. And Rick was one of those guys who, if he made $500 a month, wouldn't have a pot to piss in or if he made $500 million, wouldn't have a pot to piss in, either. Woofie would spend it, no matter what he made. That was the Woof Dog.

The Call

When Dick Phillips told me I was going up to play for the Twins, he told me not to play that night, but to get home and pack up all my stuff so I could get out the next morning. What they did let me do was take a microphone before the game and speak to my teammates and the fans. I kind of made a mess of that.

I remember going out on the field, taking the microphone and saying, "I hate to say it, but I'm upset leaving you guys here because we were going to win the league and the playoffs. Guys, go out and win this shit for me." Well, everyone kind of went "Ohhhh, nooooo, get the microphone from him," which they did.

By the end of the regular season, basically the whole team had gotten called up to another level, and Visalia didn't win the playoffs. I felt bad about that, because when we were all together, it was a heckuva team.

But I wasn't too sad to be leaving. I mean, I had achieved my biggest goal: I was heading home to play in the big leagues. It was surreal, being back at the apartment packing up to leave. The next day Dick Phillips gave me a ride to the airport. He said, "Kid, I'm going to buy you your first big-league cocktail," which was nice, except it was 10 in the morning. Dick was known to pound a few. He had his cocktail, I had a beer, and then I got on the plane to New York City for the start of my major-league career.

CHAPTER FIVE

Welcome to the Big Time

Seeing Old Friends

It's funny in baseball how things seem to go in circles. When I walked into the clubhouse in New York before my first game, about the first two people I saw were Johnny Castino and Gary Ward, neither of whom I had visited with since Instructional League.

I'd seen them from a distance in spring camp, but we were always on different fields. The A-ball guys don't hang with the AAA guys. If you're not good enough to be on their field, you don't hang with them. There's a pecking order in pro ball.

But that night in Yankee Stadium was like being back in the Instructional League with them. They gave me the best advice that anybody in this game ever gave me. Cas came over first and said, "Hrbie, it's great to see you. Just remember this game is the same game that we were playing when we were together before. It's still just baseball." Then Gary came over and said, "Great to see you, man. I'm happy for you and proud of you. But just remember, this is the same game you've played your whole life."

Right away, my mind was eased. I was 21 years old, never played a game above A-ball, and I was in Yankee Stadium. I'd never even been to a big-league ballpark other than old Met Stadium to watch the Twins as a kid. I'd never been to New York City, period. But I took their advice to heart. This was the same game I had been playing since swinging at wiffle balls in the Meyers' backyard.

First Impressions

I wasn't blown away when I first walked into Yankee Stadium. There was an aura, but the hallway leading to the clubhouse, and the clubhouse itself, had a low ceiling. I guess I expected bigger things. Of course, I hadn't seen the field yet. And after talking to Johnny and Gary, I spent about two seconds putting my uniform on. I just wanted to get down onto the field, where I figured I'd feel more at home.

When I walked onto the field, I was in awe. One second I'm at Visalia playing in a stadium that today I can't even remember the name of, the next thing I'm at Yankee Stadium. Yeah, the clubhouse in New York might have felt like a dungeon, but walking onto the field was different than anything I had ever experienced. This was the House that Babe Ruth built. You kind of felt like you were in the place where baseball had been invented. To this day, every time I walk into Yankee Stadium, I get that same feeling. It's a different feeling than any other ballpark.

Tommy John was the Yankees' starter that first game. I was 1-for-4 during the first nine innings, beating out an infield hit down the first-base line. Against a crafty lefty like John, I'll take that. At least I knew I wasn't going to be oh-for my big league career.

One thing I remember from that game is Reggie Jackson getting to first base, looking at my name on the back of my uniform and saying, "How do you say that, kid?" Then he said,

"Welcome to the big leagues, kid." Pretty nice, from a guy of his stature.

Back home in Bloomington there were parties everywhere. My parents had a group of people over, gathered around the TV. And as I later learned, a bunch of my high school buddies had parties going on too, watching the ballgame.

One For Pods

Johnny Podres was the pitching coach for the Twins in '81. I don't think it's any secret that Pods liked to have a cocktail or two. He was one of the game's great characters, and made quite a tandem along with our manager Billy Gardner, whom most people just called Slick. What a pair. Talk about funny guys with dry senses of humor.

When you walked by Pods on your way to the bat rack, he'd frequently slap you on the leg, give you a goofy look and say, "Got something goin' on tonight, Hrbie? Whatcha got goin' on?" Then he'd wink at you and laugh. I loved Pods.

As I headed to the bat rack in the 12th inning of my first big-league game, Pods hit me on the leg and said, "Hey, kid, it's getting kind of late. I'm going to need a cocktail pretty soon. Hit one out of here, will you?" I remember him saying that like it was yesterday.

Well, believe it or not, I went up and hit one out off George Frazier, who would later become a teammate of mine with the Twins. I got back to the dugout, and Pods was just sitting there, with a great big smile. He's probably loved me ever since, because I got Pods out in the big city.

About the time I got to first base I looked out to right field and saw Reggie's No. 44 with his back turned, watching the ball. It hit between the two fences, and bounced back onto the field. I thought maybe Reggie was going to save it for me, but he picked it up and tossed it into the stands. Oh well. There's some

Yankee fan out there who has my first big-league memento. But I've got the memory, and that's enough.

I got my first taste of the media that night. I walked into the clubhouse and there was a pile of people around my locker. I just wanted to get out of there, get back to the hotel and start calling everyone at home.

The whole significance of the night didn't really hit me until the year was over. I played my first game at Yankee Stadium, starting at first base where Lou Gehrig once played. And my dad was at home dying from Lou Gehrig's disease. That night, I was just living in the moment, trying to figure out how to get a hit off a guy like Tommy John. Trying to prove to the Twins that I deserved to be there. But as the years went on, that night became more and more special to me because of my dad.

Back then, as I left Yankee Stadium, all I could think about was getting back to Met Stadium and playing my first game at home. I knew my family and friends would be there to watch.

Ouch

You could say that my home debut was a little less memorable than my major-league debut. It was memorable because I got to go in the Met clubhouse for the first time, and play on the field where I'd watched the Twins as a kid. We'd go to 10 or 12 games a year, and mostly I'd go to watch Tony Oliva hit the baseball.

Tony to me was one of the greatest hitters who ever lived, and would be in the Hall of Fame if he hadn't blown out his knee. It's pretty neat that Tony and I both have our Twins numbers retired as members of the team's Hall of Fame, along with Harmon Killebrew, Rod Carew, and Kirby Puckett.

You couldn't have seen that one coming my first game at the old Met. It had been raining most of the day, and the field was wet. I don't think we even took batting practice. I did stretch, for those who are wondering, but it didn't help. Early in the game I

High school rival Timmy Laudner joined me on the Twins in late 1981.
Courtesy of the Minnesota Twins

reached for a low throw at first and blew out my hamstring. Of course I didn't want to leave the game. My parents were there, and I had a ton of friends out in the left-field stands.

Tickets weren't too hard to come by. The Twins were 41-68 that season, which was shortened because of the strike. I tried to hit one more time after feeling my hammie tear. I think I swung at the first pitch, hit a fly to center and could barely jog down the first-base line. That was it. I was out of the game.

Afterward, all my friends came up and wanted to know what happened. They didn't know I had blown out my hamstring. All they saw was me hitting a fly to center, jogging to first and then leaving the game—end of story for that night.

Greeting Friends

I missed the next two weeks before I was able to get back in the lineup. That home run in Yankee Stadium was the only one I hit that year in 67 at-bats. And I only batted .239, which wasn't very Tony Oliva-like.

But the final month of '81 was memorable for a lot of other reasons. Before the year was out, the Twins had called up a couple buddies of mine. Timmy Laudner, my old high school rival, came up from AA after hitting 42 homers at Orlando. Timmy was a catcher, not a center fielder like he had been at Park Center High. And the Twins called up G-Man, Gary Gaetti, from the same Orlando ball club.

By now Gary and I were already friends after playing a whole year at Wisconsin Rapids, and suffering through a summer under Rick "Stelly" Stelmaszek. We were pretty much instant friends in the minors. I just liked Gary's attitude. He was a guy who had no fear.

Gary hit a home run off Charlie Hough in Texas in his first big league at-bat. Everyone in the dugout was clapping, saying, "Way to go." Not me. I was screaming and hollering like a little kid.

The game was on.

CHAPTER SIX

A New Era

Home is a Dome

My rookie season in 1982 found us moving from outdoor baseball at the old Met to the Metrodome. Over the years, the building's been the target of a lot of abuse, and I understand all that. I understand it better now as a fan than I did when I played.

Back then, we were all excited to be moving into a new building. It was something brand new, and we were all so young we thought it was great. Of course, even for us reality sank in pretty quickly.

The first thing we learned was that the turf was harder than a rock. Then we learned there was no air conditioning, and it was like playing in a sweatbox. And we soon learned the fans weren't going to sit in a sweatbox and watch bad baseball.

We had more than 52,000 fans show up for our first game in the Dome, which we lost 11-7 to Seattle. The next night we had 5,213 fans show up to watch us win our first game in the building, 7-5. We had a lot of crowds like that the first year. Let me tell you, when you put 6,000 fans in that building, you can hear what the fans are saying. In an outdoor ballpark, the sound gets dispersed. In the Metrodome, it just stayed in there and resonated. You could hear a guy say, "Hey, I'll have a couple hot dogs and a beer" while you're out there trying to play the game. Do you know how hard it is to focus when the guy behind you at first base is ordering a beer and a hot dog?

When you look back at old videos from the early '80s, compared to now, you realize how empty and stark that stadium was. Not only empty stands—we had no signs, advertisements, or billboards. It was like we were playing in a warehouse. At least now there's a little activity, a little atmosphere.

We also quickly learned that the roof had a few faults...like caving in during heavy snow. It caved in during the winters of 1981 and '82, which were no big deals for us. We would read about it in the paper and just kind of chuckle. Then the same thing happened early in the 1983 season. We had a game scheduled against the Angels that night.

Gary Ward was staying with Tom Brunansky and me in Richfield until he could find an apartment for the season. Nobody planned too far ahead when it came to housing back then, because you didn't know whether you'd be packaged in a trade, or whether some minor leaguer would hit .400 in spring training and be tabbed as the next phenom and take your job. So guys roomed together the first few weeks until you had some sense of security.

Anyway, Wardo wanted to borrow my truck that morning because I had four-wheel drive. A couple hours later, I got a phone call.

"Hrbie, I'm stuck."

I said, "Wardo, you've got four-wheel drive and only eight inches of snow. You should be able to plow right through it."

And he said: "No, I'm really stuck man."

About the same time we got another call saying that the roof had collapsed, and that we were going to get the day off. We took off in Bruno's car to get Wardo out of his snowdrift. When we got there, we learned Wardo was stuck because he didn't know how to lock the hubs on the truck, which you used to have to do to get it in four-wheel drive. As soon as I locked the hubs for him, Wardo drove off through the snow. Bruno and I decided to drive down to the Dome to get a look at it. We walked in to look at the field and there was a big puddle from dripping snow behind second base.

Of course, that really wasn't unusual back in those days, because the roof leaked quite often. You'd have people watching indoor baseball, getting wet in their seats. It was kind of funny to look up and see water dripping down, and a bunch of fans get up and move out of their section, just like they would during a downpour at an outdoor ballpark.

Maybe the weirdest night we ever had in the Dome was on April 26, 1986 against the Angels. A severe thunderstorm with winds of 80 miles an hour moved through Minneapolis late in the game, and it ripped a hole in the roof over right field. It was spooky, because the lights were swinging from the ceiling and the roof was flapping. They stopped the game for nine minutes, and then we were able to finish, which wasn't exactly a good thing for us.

We had a 6-1 lead with two outs in the bottom of the eighth when the storm hit. The Angels scored six runs in the top of the ninth off Frank Viola and Ron Davis to win 7-6.

Welcome to my world.

Fixing the Problems

As the years went on, those kinds of things didn't happen anymore. They eventually installed air conditioning and figured out a way to plug the leaks in the roof. In fact over the last 20 years the Dome has been pretty good. Well...pretty good compared to the early years.

Of course, it is what it is. And it isn't your traditional baseball stadium. I've seen it all, including Dave Kingman hitting a towering pop fly that went through one of the ventilation holes in the ceiling and never came down. I've seen high pop-ups bounce off the lights, which according to the building's ground rules puts the ball in play no matter where it might have been heading.

We realized right away how hard the turf was. After a couple weeks, whenever a teammate would get a base hit to the outfield, we'd all be yelling, "Bounce." We learned that every now and then a routine one-hop single would bounce over the outfielder's head, and we realized that could be a home-field advantage for us if we could somehow anticipate it. One night Tim Teufel hit a 150-foot Texas Leaguer to right field that Harold Baines charged. The ball bounced over Baines' head, and Teufel got a three-run, inside-the-park homer to give us a 3-2 victory over the White Sox. I don't think "bounce" is a term that would have ever been used at any other ballpark, but it became part of our vocabulary.

Another word that I'm pretty certain is peculiar to the Dome is "baggie," which is what everyone calls the large rubber fence in right field. I always thought they might figure out a way to make that a wooden fence, but no, it's always been the "The Baggie." It'll always be part of the building, which maybe isn't so bad because it's unique. But then a lot about the Dome is unique.

I've seen more lost balls against the ceiling than I can count, most of them by opponents. I've always worried that someday, someone is going to get hit in the head by a high fly and it's either going to kill him or end his career.

We beat the Yankees 8-6 in a game on May 7, 1985 in which four of our runs could be attributed to balls being lost in the Dome's lights and roof. Billy Martin, the Yankee manager, went nuts after the game, saying, among many other things, "This park should be barred from baseball." The next day George Steinbrenner released a statement saying: "If I wanted my players to be ping-pong players, I would send them to China to play the Chinese National Team." The Yankees played the second game of the series under protest, which angered our manager, Billy

Gardner. Billy told the press he might protest on
Yankee Stadium, saying: "If one of my players lo:
going to say he lost it in the Big Dipper."

Overcoming Home Field

Overall, I think you'd have to say the Twins have done an
incredible job of fielding some pretty good teams lately despite
having a low budget and playing in the Metrodome.

The clubhouse has never been expanded, which means the
team has to store a lot of stuff in crates out in the hallway. You
walk downstairs in the Dome to this day and it looks like a pigsty.
You compare the Dome's clubhouse and hallways to the new,
modern stadiums and it's a joke. And yet the Twins have been in
the playoffs four out of five years since 2002, which I think is a
real credit to manger Ron Gardenhire and his coaching staff, plus
Terry Ryan and the front office. They've been able to keep the
game fun and players optimistic despite the surroundings.

Having said all that, I don't want to make it sound like I
hated playing in the Dome. In fact, I loved playing in the Dome.
Those early years I was just happy to have a uniform on and be
playing in the big leagues.

Then we started building memories, and the place really did
become home. You don't have to live in a mansion to be happy
in your home. I hit the first two home runs ever in the Dome
during an exhibition game against the Reds before the 1982
season. And then, of course, we won World Series Game 7 in
both 1987 and 1991 at the Dome. So I've got a gazillion
memories of that building.

The Twins are building a new outdoor stadium that's going
to be ready for 2010. Overall, I think that's going to be great for
the ballclub and the fans, although I've talked to people who live
a few hours away and they're worried about driving in and having
a game rained out. But that's part of the baseball experience to
me.

As a fan, I'm looking forward to the new stadium. But at the same time, it's going to be weird to know that when I walk in, I'll never have set foot on the field as a player. It'll have no personal memories for me. My memories are going to be locked in a domed stadium that might be torn down someday.

Slick and Pods

I guess the polite way of putting it would be to say we were colorful my early years with the Twins: we weren't too good; we played in a Dome; and we had quite a cast of characters, starting with Slick and Pods—manager Billy Gardner and his pitching coach Johnny Podres—and of course, Calvin Griffith, who owned the ballclub.

When your manager and pitching coach share a room at the Super 8 Motel during homestands, you know you're not playing for the Yankees. Slick was, and still is, married to the former Miss Connecticut, but she stayed out East raising their kids. I guess that said something about how Slick perceived his job security managing one of the youngest and lowest payroll teams ever to walk onto a big-league field. Slick used to joke about waking up next to Pods when he had Miss Connecticut waiting for him back home. Maybe that made him the perfect guy to manage us, because the prospect of getting fired wasn't all bad. I mean, who would you rather wake up to in your room: Miss Connecticut or The Pod?

Slick was one of the funniest guys I ever met. Problem was he talked in this thick East Coast accent, and most of the players were able to understand only about half of what he said. But that half was pretty funny. I don't know that I ever had a serious, heart-to-heart with Slick. Every time he talked to someone, he'd end the conversation with a joke that didn't always make sense. He was always telling stories.

He also kept the game simple. I don't think Billy was a strategist like Tom Kelly. Of course, part of it was I didn't

Rick Stelmaszek was one of the toughest guys I ever met as my manager at Wisconsin Rapids. He mellowed as a Twins coach, becoming a close friend. Courtesy of the Minnesota Twins

understand the game as well as I did after playing in the majors for a few years. By the time Tom Kelly had become our manager in 1987, I could look at him in the dugout and he'd make a little signal and I knew I'd have to move off the line, or whatever it was. That didn't happen with Billy. I'd look in the dugout and have no idea what was going on, other than I knew Pods wanted us to win as quickly as possible, because it got him into the night.

We got hold of a video of the final game of the 1955 World Series when Pods, pitching for Brooklyn, beat the Yankees. After the last out, Pods jumped all over the mound, then leaped into Roy Campanella's arms. We'd always ask Pods to show us that last pitch. And he always would. He'd throw a pretend pitch, then start jumping up and down in the air. And he'd always add: "Boy, we had some cocktails that night."

Rick Stelmaszek joined up with Slick and Pods at the start of the 1981 season, which made for quite an interesting group of leaders. Stelly became more like Slick and Pods as a coach than the rough and tough Chicago guy he had been as manger at Wisconsin Rapids, which was a good thing for all of us. We were a group of guys that needed humor, not ground balls hit at our heads.

Class of '82

Although we had no way of knowing it at the time, we had six rookies on our 1982 team who would be the cornerstone of the '87 World Series champions: Gary Gaetti, Tom Brunansky, Tim Laudner, Randy Bush, Frank Viola, and me. We'd have had another player on that list, but Jim Eisenreich had the misfortune of being unable to control a nervous twitch that was later diagnosed as Tourette Syndrome.

Jimmy was the Opening Day center fielder for us in '82, and he could flat-out hit. He was a country kid from St. Cloud, Minnesota, which gave us three starters from Minnesota, along with me and Lauds. None of us knew what was going on with Jimmy, other than he'd go into these terrible twitching episodes and have to leave the game. It was sad to see what happened to him in Boston when the fans got to him by yelling insults. He started to twitch and ended up running off the field to catcalls.

Jimmy tried playing for us three straight years. The guy had talent. Calvin told reporters that Eisenreich "was doomed to be an All-Star." The Twins thought it was a nervous disorder, which turned out to be a misdiagnosis. Calvin sold his contract to the Royals for $1, thinking his career was over. Jimmy got the proper diagnosis of Tourette Syndrome, went on medication to control the twitching, and ended up playing 15 years in the big leagues with a career batting average of .290. He played in the 1993 World Series with the Phillies, and won the World Series with Florida in 1997. So it turned out well.

The same could not be said for many of the players who were my teammates in the early to mid-'80s. We had a revolving door for pitchers, most of whom have long since been forgotten, except by those of us who called them teammates. One of the starters on the '82 team was Al Williams, a big right-hander who was a Nicaraguan freedom fighter during his off-seasons. At least that's what we heard. Al was pretty spooky, and you didn't mess with him. If you said anything to Al that he didn't think was funny, he'd just say, "I'll get you." So no one said much to him.

We also had Terry Felton, who lost 16 straight games with the Twins, including going 0-13 in '82. I just couldn't figure that one out, because he had some really nasty stuff. I'd face him in spring training games, and the guy had one of the best breaking balls I'd seen and a nasty fastball. Terry handled it well. He had a great sense of humor. Even during the bad times, Terry would joke around. One night we were at the apartment Brunansky and I rented in Richfield, and we heard a thump-thump-thump. It was Terry sliding down the basement stairs on his butt, having a good time. But he just couldn't win. It's not like he went out to lose. I had the feeling the guy could throw a no-hitter every time he went to the mound.

We were always searching the scrapheap for pitching help those early years. In 1985 we found Steve Howe, who had been one of the game's top relievers, but then ran into a lengthy series of drug problems. The guy was left-handed and he was breathing, so we took a shot. He had a little baggage, and we found it. He went AWOL after appearing in a few games, and that was it.

Then there was Juan Agosto, a little left-hander we picked up in 1986. Word was he was into voodoo stuff. I didn't get close enough to find out. All I know is that he was a different cat.

The guy who epitomized our pitching problems in those years was Ron Davis. We picked up RD the first week of the '82 season in a multiplayer deal with the Yankees, and RD was supposed to solidify our bullpen. It didn't quite work out that way.

That deal did, however, bring us a young shortstop named Greg Gagne. He was sent to the minors after the trade but made it to the big leagues for his first cup of coffee the next season, and was a starter on both our World Series championship teams.

We traded veteran Roy Smalley and a young pitcher named Gary "Truth" Serum to the Yankees in the deal. So even though we got RD and spent years trying to make him a closer, getting Gagne made it one of the best deals in Twins history.

Fighting Words

We lost 102 games in '82, which is the most any Twins team has ever lost. The funny thing is, we never thought of ourselves as being that bad. Losing didn't seem that hard; I guess because we were young, trying to play in the big leagues and get our feet wet. Still, we had this air about us. We weren't afraid of anybody.

I think even some of our teammates were surprised by that. Roy Smalley was one of the Twins' few veterans when I was called up in 1981. A couple years later he looked back at his first meeting with Gaetti and me while talking to a Minneapolis reporter. I think what he said is pretty accurate, and tells a lot about our frame of mind back then.

"They were the most different rookies I'd ever been around," Smalley said. "I'd never seen anything like it. Here was Hrbek, up from A-ball, and Gaetti up from AA, and they'd walk around on the field like they had the jobs and there wasn't anything to it. …I'm not saying that with any rancor. I used to laugh about it. They were brash and confident, just like they are now."

I think that air might be why we ended up having some big-time brawls in those early years, especially with Milwaukee and Detroit. I used to hit the crap out of Milwaukee, and I think that was one of the things that agitated the Brewers. Harvey Kuehn, their manager, used to stand on the top steps of the dugout screaming at me: "We're going to throw one right down the middle, Hrbek. See if you can hit this one."

The Brewers at the time were the best team in the American League, winning the Series in '82. They had a bunch of guys who had come up through their system, like Robin Yount, Paul Molitor, and Jim Gantner. And they had some real power hitters in Cecil Cooper, Gormon Thomas, and Ben Oglive.

I think, in a way, we saw ourselves in them. We were young and scuffling, but we were going to learn the game together and someday be like the Brewers. I think from the Brewers' perspective maybe we were a little too cocky in that belief, and didn't show them the respect they figured they deserved.

The first big brawl started when our center fielder, Bobby Mitchell, slid hard into second and took out Yount. I guess maybe they thought Yount shouldn't be treated like that. Well, a couple innings later one of the Brewers basically veered into the outfield to get our shortstop, Lenny Faedo, and knocked him into next week. I was standing on first watching, and the next thing I know the whole Brewers dugout was running toward me, and I was heading toward right field.

My mom and grandmother were at the game, and my mom told me later that my grandmother turned to her and said, "I sure hope Kent didn't get hurt." Well, they beat the hell out of me. I can still remember Ted Simmons on top of me, punching on me. There was a picture of me in the paper the next day after the fight. I'm carrying one shoe, my hat is off, and I've got no glove. I wasn't even mouthy to the Brewers. They just didn't care for me.

We had problems with the Brewers right up to 1987. We had a brawl that year, too, when they threw Joe Niekro on the ground and hurt his shoulder. That was the tail end of our fighting years with the Brewers.

We might have been losing games, but there were signs that things were going to turn someday. I hit .301 with 23 homers, drove in 92 runs, and finished second in Rookie of the Year voting to Cal Ripken. G-Man hit 25 homers and Brunansky hit 20. Not bad for rookies. Problem was: We continued to hold tryouts, trying to find pitchers who could get anybody out. One guy who showed some promise was Viola, although he had to learn on the job like the rest of us, going 4-10 with a 5.21 ERA in his first major-league season.

CHAPTER SEVEN

G-Man

Like My Brother

Gary Gaetti was like a brother to me. That's no exaggeration. We grew up together as professionals—spending a year together at Wisconsin Rapids in Class-A ball; hitting our first big-league homers late in 1981; and losing 102 games together as rookies in '82. Maybe it was all that losing that made us so close. One thing we had in common, maybe more than anything else, was that we hated to lose.

Tom Kelly told people at various times that there was no one on the team who wanted to win more than Kent Hrbek. I took a lot of pride in that. I hated every opponent, and I absolutely hated to lose. G-Man was the same way, and I liked that about him from the first time we met.

Gary would walk up on the top dugout step and scream obscenities at the opposing pitcher. There were times he'd strike out on three curve balls in the dirt, stomp back to the dugout and yell at the pitcher that he was chicken shit for not having the guts to throw a fastball. Gary didn't think much of a pitcher's manliness if he had to rely on a curveball, rather than go toe-to-toe with a fastball.

Gary would even scream at our own pitchers when he felt they had thrown the wrong pitch. You can see that to this day in the video from Game 6 of the '87 World Series. One of our pitchers gave up a hit, and you can see Gary kicking the dirt and cussing in the background.

Some writers described Gary as the heart and soul of our team in the '80s. In a lot of ways, he was our leader. He had this Italian name, could grow a beard in half an hour, and grew up as this tough guy. He was a couple years older than me, and I always felt I could learn something from him.

Roomies

We roomed together on the road from our rookie year pretty much until late in the 1980s. It wasn't cool to have a road roommate in those years. If you made enough money, most guys would get a single room.

Gary and I didn't think that way. We liked rooming together. Not only could we save a little money, but we had someone to talk to at night. Many nights we'd be going over the games long after we shut the lights out. That year we lost 102 games, it seemed like every stinking night we'd go back to the room and talk about what we could have done better.

The one thing we almost never talked about was each other's hitting, because we were so different as hitters. Gary tried to guess on every pitch, and that's why he looked so stupid sometimes. But if he guessed right on a fastball, look out. I tried to pick up every pitch as it was released. I always felt like I could pick up the spin. I'd try to see the curveball coming out of the pitcher's hand, because most pitchers pop up their hand a little more throwing a curve than a fastball. So we were on different wavelengths, and we left that subject alone.

Two of my best friends in baseball were Gary Gaetti (left) and Randy Bush (right). Courtesy of the Minnesota Twins

But we talked a lot of other baseball, and a lot of life in general. On the days we lost, we'd both be pissed off. A lot of times we'd go take it out on a bottle of beer or a glass of whiskey. We laughed together, drank a few pops and cocktails together and sometimes got drunker than hell together. Through it all, I watched his back, and I knew he'd be there to watch mine.

All or Nothing

Gary was a little different in his approach than most guys, not only to baseball but life in general. When he dove into something, he'd go all the way up to his neck. He wasn't a guy who touched the water with his toe before going in. He just jumped.

One example was when Roy Smalley brought this eat-to-win thing into the clubhouse. Well, Gary dove into that. Pretty soon, he was totally into the diet, even more than Smalley. Another time, Gary started going to a sports psychologist, and he became convinced that focus was the key to success.

Well, in 1988, Gary found religion. That came about shortly after we traded Tom Brunansky to the Cardinals for Tommy Herr, who is probably the only guy I played with whom I really didn't like as a teammate. Herr was a born-again Christian, and spent most of his time in the clubhouse sitting in front of his locker, reading the Bible. Gary's locker was next to Herr's, and by the end of the year Gary was sitting in front of his locker, reading the Bible.

But I didn't dislike Tommy Herr because he helped convert G-Man. I disliked Herr because he didn't want to be here. He got off the plane in Minneapolis the night of the trade and told people he'd been crying over leaving the Cardinals. He never did seem like he wanted to be here, and he just didn't fit in with us. That's why I didn't like Tommy Herr.

The religion was Gary's choice, not Herr's. What got to me—and what changed our relationship—was that Gary started preaching to me. I honestly didn't care what Gary was into, or what he believed in, but I didn't want him preaching to me.

He said some goofy things, like telling me that if I kept drinking beer, I was going to hell. Now, isn't that the pot calling the kettle black? I said, "Gary, the same thing you were doing with me last year—running around, having a good time, closing up bars—now I'm going to hell because of it? And you're not?" I never understood that. But Gary was convinced, even more so than he had been on diets and sports psychologists.

The summer of 1988 was a long one. It was like Gary Gaetti had died—at least the Gary Gaetti I knew. One day he was one person, the next day he was someone else. It was almost that quick.

Gary got involved with some people who were almost like a cult, and they had people in every city. We were still rooming together on the road, and there were nights Gary wouldn't come back to the room because he'd be with some group talking religion all night. He'd show up in the clubhouse half an hour before batting practice, grab his Bible and start reading.

It changed our clubhouse. I know it hurt TK, too. TK lost his fiery third baseman, the one who would be screaming at the opponent from the top steps of the dugout after striking out. Now when he struck out, he'd just walk back to the dugout, place his bat back in the rack and sit down. All of a sudden everybody, including the opponent, was good. And if you didn't do it his way, you were going to hell.

We had other guys who were into religion big-time back them. Greg Gagne was, but he didn't preach to others. I had no problem at all with Gags. Brian Harper preached a little. Tommy Herr mostly just sat there and read his Bible. To each his own. I just didn't like being preached to.

The End Wasn't Near

But we were able to have a little fun with most of the guys who got into religion, even on the subject of religion. We had a road trip to Seattle that coincided with what some people thought was going to be the end of the world. Everybody thought they were going to be blasted off to heaven—they believed that was literally going to happen. Gagne and Harper brought their wives on the trip, because they were so sure the end of the world was upon us.

Our clubhouse guy was Jimmy Wiesner, another guy I loved because he absolutely hated the opponent. I looked over in the dugout on the day all this was supposed to happen, and Wiesner had a batting helmet on. That was weird, even for Jimmy. He never even wore a hat. When I asked him why he had a helmet on, he said, "Well, if I'm going to take off straight to heaven, I'm going to be going through the roof of the Kingdome, and I'm going to hit my head like hell." Wiesey was always a guy who could jab any player on the team.

Everybody took the joking well, and laughed. By the end of the day we were all still on earth, and the guys were back reading their Bibles trying to figure out how the whole thing had been messed up.

But with G-Man it got to the point that year where things became sticky. You couldn't mess with him. G-Man started getting angry when you joked around, and you had to watch what you said.

So that was the year it was like I lost my brother, like I had suffered another death in the family. That's the only way I know how to describe it. The fire that G-Man brought to the team—that fire that had helped us win the World Series in 1987—just went out.

G-Man Departs

At the end of the 1990 season, the Twins didn't make much of an effort to re-sign Gaetti. So he left as a free agent and signed with the Angels. I think everybody felt a change of scenery would be best for both Gary and the team. Since 1988, when we won 91 games, our record had steadily declined to 78-84 in 1990.

Obviously we had other problems those years than Gary's conversion. The Herr trade was a fiasco, and the Twins packaged him in a trade after the '88 season for left-hander Shane Rawley, who was 5-12 with an equally bad ERA in his only season.

By the time the 1990 season ended, things were better between Gary and me. I think we just learned to accept that this was the way things were. He went his way; I went mine. I certainly didn't hate him. When he decided to leave, it wasn't like I was pushing for the Twins to get rid of him. We were past all that stuff.

We talked about the preaching, and that got patched up. I'm not a guy who gives too many people second chances, but I did with him. Just like you'd give your brother a second chance. I loved the guy.

After he left, I rooted for him. Not when he played the Twins, of course. But the other times I sure did.

A couple years later he kind of chilled out a little. He even had a beer now and then, which was funny, because it kind of became big news around our club. Geez, did you hear G-Man was seen having a beer? Like I'd never seen that before.

We've been hunting a few times after that. We've laughed, told stories, had a heater or two and sipped a few beers.

Almost like old times.

CHAPTER EIGHT

Moving Up

Still Learning

After our 102-loss season as rookies in 1982, things got a little better. Not overnight, mind you. In 1983 we took a baby step, winning 10 more games to finish 70-92. Tom Brunansky, Gary Gaetti, and I combined for 65 homers. But once again we had trouble getting anyone out. We kept searching through baseball's scrap heap, trying to sign guys who had been released or pick up someone with a little promise in a low-profile trade.

We got lucky in Ken Schrom, who had been released by Toronto after the 1982 season. All getting released meant was that Schrom was good enough to start for us, and led the staff with 15 victories in '83. He was also a new fishing buddy for me, a good guy who was one of the few pitchers I really got to know well early in my career. Most of the others were, well, a little different. You didn't talk to them on days they pitched, stuff like that.

But Schrom was different. He gave us a ray of hope. We even ended up rooming together on the road for a while in '84. I wasn't married yet, and Debby Gaetti told Gary she didn't want

During spring training in 1983, I mug for the camera.
Courtesy of the Minnesota Twins

him rooming with me. I guess she thought I liked to party a little too much, although I'd like to note for the record that Debby lifted her ban after I married Jeanie in 1985.

Anyway, Schrom and Big Al Williams were the only guys on our staff with more than 10 victories in 1983. We had 10 different pitchers start at least four games. Frankie Viola led our staff with 34 starts, but he was still learning on the job, as his 7-15 record and his 5.49 ERA showed.

It took a while for Frankie to mature into a great pitcher, which as I look back doesn't surprise me. He was one of the most nervous pitchers I've ever been around. I don't remember why, but on a road trip to Oakland I ended up rooming with Frankie. Big mistake. He was up all night—didn't sleep a wink. Every time there'd be a noise in the parking lot, Frankie would jump out of bed and run to the window. Finally I said, "Frankie, at least stay in bed. I've got to play tomorrow, too."

That was the last time I ever shared a room with Frank Viola.

First Taste

We thought we turned the corner in 1984. We were in the race with the Royals until the final week, thanks in large part to an off-season deal in which one of our few veteran players, Gary Ward, was traded to Texas for three players, including starting pitchers John Butcher and Mike Smithson. Butcher and Smithson were legitimate major-league pitchers, something we hadn't seen a whole lot of since I joined the Twins. It gave us a little hope. For once we weren't searching the scrap heap for pitchers. We traded a quality hitter and got a couple pitchers who had some numbers and some time in the big leagues.

We kind of snuck up on people. We started fairly slow, going over .500 for the first time in six weeks at 40-39 when we beat Baltimore 3-1. Then we ended July with a five-game winning streak, winning 9-2 on the last day of the month against Seattle to improve our record to 54-49.

When we swept a doubleheader at Milwaukee on August 22, we were 67-58, and people were starting to take notice. We won five straight again, and on September 24 we were 81-75, just a half-game behind a veteran Kansas City club that was 82-75. The Royals had won the AL West Division four times since 1976 and had been in the race every other season. They kept talking about how tough it was for a team to win the first time it experienced a pennant race.

We proved 'em right, that's for sure. We lost our final six games, including two that rank among the most memorable losses in Twins history. We lost the final two games of a series against the White Sox, then went to Cleveland for a season-ending four-game series. We were still only 1 1/2 games behind the Royals, and a game in the loss column, when we arrived in Cleveland. Ron Davis entered the opening game of the Cleveland series with a runner on first, one out and a 3-1 lead in the bottom of the eighth. He gave up two runs, tying the game. The next inning Jamie Quirk hit a two-out, walk-off homer, which was pretty unexpected since it came in Quirk's only at-bat ever with Cleveland.

That was nothing compared to the next night, when we took a 10-0 lead in the top of the third with Viola on the mound. We still had a 10-2 lead, before Cleveland scored seven runs in the bottom of the sixth. RD took the mound in the eighth to protect that 10-9 lead. He gave up a homer to Joe Carter to tie the game, then walked two of the first three batters he faced in the ninth. Billy Gardner mercifully removed him, but Eddie Hodge gave up a game-winning hit and we lost 11-10. That loss eliminated us from the race, putting us three games behind the Royals with two games to play.

At least that night produced one of the most memorable quotes in Twins history. Gaetti had a critical throwing error during Cleveland's seven-run sixth inning, and after the game he told a Minneapolis reporter: "It's hard to throw to first base with both hands around your neck." That was G-Man, being painfully honest. We choked, and he had the guts to acknowledge it.

I don't spend a lot of time thinking about '84, because what we did in '87 and '91 overshadowed the disappointment. I think the '84 season caught a lot of us by surprise, and even caught the fans by surprise. To this day I don't remember a lot from that season, other than Jamie Quirk and blowing a 10-0 lead—and the fact that I had a darn good season.

Numbers-wise it was my best year. I hit .311 with 27 homers and 107 RBIs. But you know how a lot of people don't believe a pitcher should be considered an MVP candidate, being that they have their own award—the Cy Young? Well, they gave the MVP award to Detroit reliever Willie Hernandez. My rookie season, when I hit .301 and drove in 92 runs, I finished second to Cal Ripken for Rookie of the Year. I guess I'm just a second-place kind of guy when it comes to awards. But I never finished second in the World Series, did I?

Farewell

The 1984 season was an important one in Twins history for reasons that extended beyond our run at the pennant. It was the year that Calvin Griffith sold the club to Carl Pohlad, and the year that a rookie named Kirby Puckett took over as the Twins' center fielder. Calvin is a huge part of baseball's history, and I always had a warm spot for him. He was the guy who brought major-league baseball to Minnesota when he moved the Washington Senators to the Twin Cities in 1961.

Calvin was the last of the Great Mohicans, the only guy running baseball as a family business in the 1980s without a billion-dollar business to back him up. Everyone always said Calvin was cheap, Calvin was this, Calvin was that. Calvin just didn't have the finances to do much, and I understood his position. I never was one to spend a lot of time worrying about what we didn't have. That was ownership and the front office. My job was to play baseball, period.

I think it hurt him to death when he sold the team. It probably killed him. He loved the game. It was his whole life. Late in his life he moved to Helena, Montana, and I heard he showed up every night to watch the Class A team play in the Northwest League. Calvin Griffith just plain loved baseball.

After I finished playing in the minor leagues at Wisconsin Rapids in 1980 I got to visit Met Stadium and meet Calvin. Angelo Guiliani, the scout who signed me, brought me into his office and said, "This is Kent Hrbek, the kid from Bloomington that we signed. He's playing in the minors now." Calvin was eating a bowl of tomato soup at the time, and he had this napkin tucked in his shirt. On that day he had tomato soup all over his napkin. He just looked up from his soup and said something to the effect of: "You're a pretty big kid. Just get out there and hit the ball hard."

That was Calvin: no airs about him—just a regular guy who happened to own a baseball team. Every time I saw him in a hallway at the ballpark I'd say, "Hi, Mr. Griffith." I had a lot of respect for the man. I thank the guy a million times for giving me a chance. I'll tell you, the guy could find talent, right up to the end.

And when we won the pennant in '87, I think he took a lot of pride in that, because the core of that team—me, G-Man, Kirby Puckett, Brunansky, Tim Laudner, Randy Bush, and Viola—was a product of his farm system. We all felt that Calvin was a big part of that victory.

Hello

Kirby Puckett was typical of the way the Griffith organization found talent. Puckett wasn't drafted out of high school, and worked some manual-labor jobs before getting into Triton Junior College in Chicago. He played summer ball in

The 1986 crew included (from left) Tom Brunansky, Roy Smalley, Kirby Puckett, Gary Gaetti and me. Courtesy of the Minnesota Twins

Chicago with the son of Jim Rantz, the Twins' longtime minor-league director. Rantz was in the stands to watch his son, took a liking to Puckett, and the Twins drafted him in the secondary phase of the draft for undrafted college players.

It made for a great story, like much of Puck's life. He was the best player I've ever seen, or played with. But I'll be honest: I was never close to Puck. All the years we played we never went out to dinner alone together or sat in the same fishing boat.

That'll surprise some people, because Puck talked quite a bit about fishing with me, and often made it sound like we were best friends. It was like if you saw Hrbie, you expected to see Kirby. Hrbie and Kirby. The Twins put out a poster of us one year, and I guess it made for good marketing. It just wasn't the way it was.

Puck did some things that bothered me, one of them being that he would always be visiting with the opposing players before games. Puck would walk on the field, and the whole team would come over to talk to him. That always burned my crank. My feelings were you didn't socialize with the other team. I talked with him a couple times about that. I told him, we're trying to whoop that guy's ass, you can't be friends with him. And if you want to be his friend, do it off the field.

But Puck had his own way of doing things. He loved the attention. One of the stories you hear over and over about Puck is how he told his teammates before Game 6 of the 1991 World Series to jump on his back, that he was driving the bus tonight. Well, Puck said that before every game he ever played. Every time he left the clubhouse he said, "Jump on my back. I'm driving the bus tonight." We used to laugh at that. Randy Bush would check the lineup card, see that his name wasn't on it and yell out, "Jump on my back tonight, guys. I'm driving the bus." I'd say, "I don't want anyone on my back tonight, because I'm too fat and I'm too sore." We'd all laugh at that stuff, including Puck. But then it became part of Puck's legend. And Puck didn't mind being legendary.

In the end, I think we all learned how tough it is to be a legend. The media loved Puck, and they put him on a pedestal. Then after he retired he went through a very public divorce and some nasty things stuff came out about him. But people didn't want to believe negative things about Puck. They still wanted him on that pedestal, and that's pretty tough for anyone to live up to.

When the Twins didn't rehire him as a vice president after some of his problems became public, it hurt him. It hurt the Twins, too, but it was a decision that had to be made, the way things were going. I honestly think that was the first time in Kirby's life that someone said no to him. Kirby moved to Arizona after that. For Kirby to leave Minnesota when he once had the whole state in the palm of his hand, I think it ended up costing him his life. He got in way too deep with partying, and he didn't have anyone to steer him.

A lot of times it's much tougher to be forced to quit the game than to retire and leave on your own terms like I did. We all knew how much it hurt Puck when his career ended in the spring of 1996 because of glaucoma. I don't think he ever let on how much he missed it. But I think we all know now.

CHAPTER NINE

A Step Back

Whatever optimism we generated in 1984 evaporated quickly the following season when we lost nine of our first 11 games. You could almost hear the fans saying, "Same old Twins." We did put together a 10-game winning streak at the end of May to get over .500, but that proved only temporary. We lost 10 straight at the end of May, and never got back over .500.

If you're looking for someone who symbolized that season, try a young left-handed reliever named Tom Klawitter, better known as "The Klaw." Now, on a legitimate pennant contender, The Klaw wouldn't have been considered the answer to your left-handed relief problems. He'd pitched in Class-A ball the year before, and should have been in camp getting a little experience.

But The Klaw quickly worked his way into the team's bullpen plans, which should have been a clue for us that we might not be ready to be a serious contender. Plus, RD—Ron Davis—was back as closer after the demoralizing final week in Cleveland in '84.

It seemed like we always had some phenom in spring training who would put up fantastic numbers and we'd give him a shot in the majors. That was the state of our pitching staff back then.

Klaw became something of a cult hero during spring training, with the help of our manager. When Billy Gardner walked out to the mound to signal him in, he'd put his hand in the air and make a claw sign. That was kind of a fun thing to do.

Klaw seemed like a nice guy. We were asking him to make the jump from A ball, but some guys do it. I had done it myself. But The Klaw didn't make it. The start of the '85 season was his one and only in the big leagues, mostly because he walked 13 in 9 1/3 innings. I think he had a little "light standarditis," as Rick Stelmaszek calls it. The light towers seem taller, and a lot of people get more scared and nervous. We saw a lot of that in those years. You'd see minor leaguers with great talent, but when they got to the majors they didn't have something. Maybe part of that was the makeup of our team, because most of us were still so young, we really didn't have anyone to lead the way when a young guy started struggling.

In terms of experience and age, left fielder Mickey Hatcher was one of our veteran leaders. Hatch played the game hard, and got the most out of his ability, but he was a little off the wall to be a father figure to struggling youngsters. One day in Oakland he settled under a towering fly ball, and we're all thinking, "Good, there's another out for us." Then his knees started shaking, and he dropped to the ground, like he had fainted. Of course he didn't catch the ball. They took Hatch in for a brain scan, but I guess the old joke that the scan showed nothing applied to what they found in Hatch's brain. None of the players were too concerned awaiting the test results, because some of the guys knew that Hatch had been out the night before and had a little too much to drink. We figured, correctly, that he was just dehydrated, and got dizzy trying to track that fly ball.

That's the way things went for us back then.

Goodbye Billy

Our failure to build on '84 cost Billy Gardner his job. I hated to see him go, although I'm not sure I ever knew Billy real well. He was the nicest guy in the world, and he probably did as well as anyone could with the talent on hand. We had the core group of guys who had come in together as rookies in '82, but beyond that it seemed like there were guys coming in and out all the time, and we had no idea who we'd have on the team the next week.

I had a hand in Billy being fired, because I struggled big time the first two months of 1985. I was hitting .211 at the end of April, and .249 when Billy was fired in mid-June. It was probably the toughest two months hitting I've ever had. I know I put on a face at the ballpark to try not to show things were bothering me. But that ate at me. There was a newspaper article in 1986 where Jeanie talked about that period, saying: "After a game last year, the first thing he'd say was, 'I'm not going to let it bother me.' But a half-hour later he'd be asking me, 'Jeanie, what am I doing wrong?' He'd always be going over videotapes of himself batting, trying to figure it out."

Jeanie wasn't misquoted, let's put it that way. I did struggle. I think it might have been easier for me if my dad had been alive. He'd watched me play since I was a little kid, and when I needed someone to talk to about hitting, he was the guy. As the years went on, I talked more and more baseball with my mom. A couple of times, she made suggestions in my stance that I tried. And a couple times, they worked. But during 1985, I missed having my dad to talk to.

The best thing I learned from Billy Gardner was the same thing I learned in high school from Buster Radebach: The game has to be fun. Play it hard, play to win, but have fun.

Billy got canned in June when we were 27-35, and was replaced by Ray Miller, who had built a name for himself as the pitching coach with Baltimore. Hiring Ray seemed like a good idea for a team that needed to upgrade its pitching. And we did play .500 ball after Ray was hired in '85, so some people thought we were headed in the right direction.

But in the end, Ray's stint with the Twins didn't turn out a whole lot better than The Klaw's. Ray got canned late in the '86 season with our record at 59-80. Ray never did solve our pitching problems, and he didn't build much of a rapport with the everyday players. I liked Ray as a person, but as a manager he really didn't do much to build any chemistry in the clubhouse. Plus he put a ban on fishing when he told us to stay out of the sun. I just don't think he thought that one through. Did that mean you shouldn't be playing in the backyard with your kids because you could get sunburned?

Ray was a guy who liked being a manager, if you know what I mean. He liked sitting in his manager's office, talking to the media about the game. Even while he was the manager, the guy who was working the clubhouse, getting to know the players and building relationships, was Tom Kelly.

TK was named the interim manager when Ray was fired. The choice for a permanent manager dragged out for months during the off-season. We had a young general manager, Andy MacPhail, who was in TK's corner. But our owner, Mr. Pohlad, appeared to favor a more veteran manager like Jim Frey, who had been the manager of the Chicago Cubs.

I lobbied hard for TK. I thought he'd be perfect. I'd never played a full season for him as manager, but he had been our third-base coach and he knew the players. Plus he had managed Tim Laudner, Gary Gaetti, Randy Bush and Frank Viola in the minors, and they all had a good relationship with him. Tom Kelly was already in our clubhouse, and he knew the personalities. Why go outside the organization when it's going to take another half year to get to know the personalities?

TK finally got the job, which was a relief.

The Trade

Ray Miller did make one lasting contribution to the Twins: He moved RD from the closer's role, and was manager when RD was traded to the Cubs on August 13, 1986. There are some people who think that date was a turning point in Twins history. I don't buy it. People wrote that RD was a cancer, and that was horrible.

RD had a heart bigger than his chest, and he was a great teammate. I'm not going to deny that he did things that got some people angry, like singing that damn tune, "Jimmy Crack Corn," after a loss. He also was known to trade baseballs for bratwurst sitting in the bullpen in Milwaukee. I heard that and I got a little angry, because we're out there busting our butts to try to win a game, and RD is eating brats in the bullpen. But you know what? If I had been out there in the bullpen, I'd have probably been eating brats, too, so I forgave him.

RD gave us everything he had, which when it came to closing games wasn't enough. It got to the point where something had to be done. Miller took RD out of the closer's role fairly early in the year, which basically left us without a proven closer. Keith Atherton, a veteran long reliever, led us with 10 saves that year. But there were games when Ray would have to turn to RD simply because he'd run out of pitchers.

The night before he was traded, RD lost an extra-inning game in California. RD's ERA at the time was over 9.00, and things were so bad that night that he sat in front of his locker and cried. A reporter asked Miller if, despite the loss, he felt sorry for RD. Ray looked up and said: "Do you ever feel sorry for me? My future depends on a reliever who's sitting in front of his locker right now crying."

Well, that pretty much summed up the state of things. The next day RD was traded to the Cubs, and I don't think we reacted too well. The charter flight from California to Seattle turned into a party. People got a little goofy. Puck kind of started it by singing

"Jimmy Crack Corn" as he got on the bus to the airport. And the singing continued for most of the flight to Seattle. Puck went nuts with it. People started laughing at Puck, and when Puck got the floor, he didn't give it up. Harmon Killebrew, who was a TV analyst at the time, said it was the most bizarre thing he'd ever seen in baseball. He said it was like the team had been exorcized of a demon.

The way we acted, I can sure understand why Harmon thought that. I don't think we did ourselves proud that night. I'll always remember RD as a good teammate and friend, and the guy who had the balls to clean fish in the trainer's room.

The Off-Season

MacPhail started putting his stamp on the club during that off-season with one of the best trades in team history. We sent Neal Heaton, a veteran pitcher, Yorkis Perez, a promising young pitcher and catcher Jeff Reed to the Expos for closer Jeff Reardon and catcher Tom Nieto. Three weeks later we made another deal with the Expos to bring in veteran infielder Al Newman. All three helped us win the AL West in '87, but the key of course was Reardon.

All of a sudden we went from having no proven closer to having Jeff Reardon, who had already established himself as one of the best in the game. Jeff was a National League All-Star in '85 and '86, and saved 76 games those two years. So on paper, that was a deal that looked pretty good for us.

But the honest truth is I didn't feel any different when February rolled around in 1987 than I did starting to think about spring training any other year. I got excited every off-season, and every year when I went to spring training I thought we were going to win. That's just the way my mind works. Reardon was a great trade, but when we got Ron Davis from the Yankees in 1982 I got jacked up—we were getting a guy who was good enough to pitch for the Yankees.

I just always believed we could win. I loved the uncertainty of baseball, because you never knew what could happen. Sometimes in baseball what looks like a minor deal turns out to be huge. Like the year we signed Kenny Schrom after he got released from Toronto, and he went out and won 15 games.

If you're going to play this game, you have to have that kind of positive attitude. If you start getting down, and doubting yourself or your teammates, you've got no chance. I used to have some killer batting slumps, and it's natural that some negative thoughts start creeping in. But you've got to push them out, because if you don't, it will eat you up. If you dwell on it, and think about it all day long, it can only make things worse.

And there were people that did. Scotty Leius, a third baseman with us in the early 1990s, always thought he was going to be released. Scotty was a heckuva player, but he was a worrier, and that might have prevented him from being the player he could have been. Another guy like that was Pat Mahomes, a young pitcher who had all the talent in the world when he joined the club in '92. But you'd go to the mound and talk to him, and he was scared to death. He'd look right through you like he couldn't even see you. Here was a guy with as much talent as I've ever seen in my life—great arm, had a vertical jump like you couldn't believe, a nice, sincere kid—and he was scared to death. You could tell on the mound that the doubts were creeping in, and he really didn't believe he could do it.

I don't know enough about the brain to know why some guys think that way, and others are able to push their negative thoughts out. I just know I was lucky enough to be a guy who could push negative thoughts out. Maybe it came from having my dad die when I was 21. I'm not the only guy that's happened to, so I don't feel sorry for myself. What it taught me was to stay positive and enjoy today, because you don't know what's going to happen tomorrow.

I'm the same way when I'm fishing. I've fished with people who, when we don't get a bite for a while, will start talking about how the wind has changed and we're not going to get anything today. Hey, you hold a cheeseburger in front of my face long enough and I'm going to eat it. I always figured fish were the same way. I figured I could make 'em bite if I held food in front of their noses long enough.

So when I went to spring training in 1987, it was no different than going any other year. I was excited, and I believed we were going to win. Of course, I'd been proven wrong before. Every year I'd played in the big leagues, in fact.

CHAPTER TEN

The New Pieces

E ars full of shaving cream and burning shoelaces.
Those are two of my favorite memories from the 1987 regular season.

On the field it was a little like '84, where we kind of snuck up on people. We sure didn't blow anybody away. We couldn't win on the road, we had two quality starting pitchers and overall we had just 87 victories. But we played in a weak division, and it was enough to get us into the playoffs.

Once again we had some real characters on that team, the difference from previous years being that the characters also had a little more ability when it came to baseball. Take Bert Blyleven. Some might add "Please" after that, since Bert could drive you nuts.

His main gig was burning people's shoelaces. One time in '87, during a game, he crawled all the way under the dugout bench, from one end to the other, and lit manager Tom Kelly's shoelaces on fire. I thought it was pretty neat to be on a team where a player would feel comfortable enough to do that to his manager. TK would take that sort of thing, but you knew where the line was with him, and you didn't go over it. But his line was pretty high, as long as you were giving him everything you had on the field.

Bert could be a pain in the ass, because every time he'd burn your shoelaces you'd have to put new ones back in, and that took a lot of time. And Bert taught a lot of guys on the team how to burn shoelaces, so you always had to be alert. If they got you, you usually ended up giving the clubhouse guys a couple dollars to put new shoelaces back in. We probably had some of the best-paid clubhouse guys in the league, thanks to Bert and his followers.

Our other main schtick as a team was planting shaving cream in the ear end of the telephone. We did that one all the time. So much, in fact, that you'd often refuse to answer a phone when someone yelled that you had a call. But that would only get the guys doing the trick more determined. So they'd go get our trainer, Dick Martin, to yell out that you had a phone call. Well, when Dick called for you it was usually important, so you'd let your guard down, run into the trainer's room and grab the phone. And get an ear full of shaving cream.

There wasn't a person in the clubhouse who didn't get busted with shaving cream. It was stupid, but it kept us loose. And there wasn't a guy on the team who took it to heart and didn't have fun with it.

To me, that was a really important reason that we had the success we did in '87. I've always been a big believer in intangibles, and if you're all pulling the same way—from the front office to the clubhouse guys—I think that makes a huge difference. A successful team can't have anyone bitching about the front office or the traveling secretary. When you've got everyone on the same page within an organization, that gives you a chance to hit your peak. You get just one person off the page, and that makes a difference. I honestly believe one person can pull a whole team down.

Of course, there was more to our success in '87 than practical jokes. One big reason was that the front office made some major

As it turned out, Tom Brunansky (left), Kirby Puckett (second from right), Gary Gaetti (right) and I were the right combination of talent needed for the Twins to win a World Series. Courtesy of the Minnesota Twins

changes before the '87 season. We got an All-Star closer in Jeff Reardon, a set-up man in Juan Berenguer, a leadoff hitter and left fielder in Danny Gladden, and a top bench player in Al Newman. The new guys fit in, probably better than anyone had a right to anticipate. And as an added bonus, they could play a little bit. That always helps.

The Terminator

The key addition was Reardon. Although I hate it when people blame Ron Davis for our early problems, the truth is we struggled for years to find a closer. Getting Reardon was about the first time we went out and acquired somebody who still had something left, instead of getting someone who was washed up and nobody else wanted. When we acquired Reardon, we immediately had confidence that if we could get a lead into the late innings, we had a shot to win. That's a huge mind-set for a team to have.

The impressive thing about Jeff is that he struggled big-time the first two months of the season. By late May he had an ERA over 10.00 and was struggling with his control. As a team, we were under .500, at 21-22. But Jeff kept asking for the ball. He didn't change a bit, even when he was struggling, and I think we all gained a lot of respect for him those first two months.

Of course, the thing with Reardon is that I don't think any of us had a read on what was going on inside of him. We called him "The Terminator," or "Yak," because of his big curveball that we called a yakker. I always said he looked like Charlie Manson. He was a little spooky looking with that beard and those steely eyes. Charlie Manson probably isn't a guy you want to be associated with, and I said it just for fun, but he had that look.

Beneath the beard was a guy who was extremely quiet and shy. Nicest guy in the world, but you just didn't talk to Term much. In fact, that whole 1987 season, I never had a long conversation with him. He always had this little laugh: "heh, heh,

heh." You'd be talking to him, and he'd give you that little, "heh, heh, heh," and turn and walk away.

A lot of closers are a little different. Maybe a little bit like kickers and punters in football. They have their own routine to get ready for a game, and keep to themselves a lot.

Later in life Term ran into some real problems. He had a son who died a few years ago, and after that Term ran into some heart problems and some psychological problems. I couldn't believe when I heard the news that he'd been arrested for robbing a jewelry story in Florida. I knew he was a guy who would never do anything like that, and that's what came out. He was on medication for his heart and depression and it affected his mental state to the point where he apparently didn't even know what he was doing.

I'm rooting for Term to get his life back in order, because he's a great guy—a very sincere, sensitive guy. He might look like a guy who's going to grab the neighbor's cat and squeeze its head off. But Term would be the guy holding the cat and petting it.

Señor Smoke

Have you ever seen those cartoons where you see the bull with a ring in his nose, scratching the ground with his hoof, snorting fire? Every time I see one of those cartoon bulls, I think of Juan Berenguer, because that's what he was like on the mound.

He was "Señor Smoke." He'd no more than get the ball back from the catcher and he'd be ready to throw it again. He was always jacked up on the mound, because he just loved to get people out. I know during the playoffs in '87 some people felt he was showing the Tigers up with his arm pump, and I hated to see it, but there was nothing you could do about it. That was Juanie just being pumped up—funny, colorful and a little bit moody. But I loved watching the guy pitch.

One thing that added to Juanie's persona is that he never really mastered the complete English language. He used to butcher little parts of it. Like instead of saying "son of a bitch," Juanie would always say "son of my bitch."

I know firsthand. On one of our road trips during the regular season our charter landed late and the team bus got to our hotel in Toronto about 4 a.m. We were going through the hotel's revolving door, all of us tired as heck, just shuffling along. I had Juanie going through the door right behind me, carrying his briefcase, like he always did, and wearing one of those funny little Fedora hats. As I was going through the door, I did one of those quick stops, just to see if he was awake. He wasn't.

His face ran right into the glass door. I looked back, and all I could see was Juanie's nose, mustache and big teeth planted against the glass. We got out of the door and Juanie chased me all over the lobby, screaming, "You son of my bitch! You son of my bitch!"

The funniest thing was going down the next day and seeing Juanie's big nose print still plastered on the revolving glass door.

But what a great guy to have on your staff. Juan would have pitched every day if they let him. One of the classic interviews was Juanie talking after Game 6 of the '87 Series. The reporter asked Juan if he'd be able to pitch tomorrow, and Juan didn't hesitate: "I pitch tomorrow. I start tomorrow if they need me." He was a classic. His arm always hurt him, but he'd throw until it fell off. He loved pitching that much.

Newmie

We picked up Al Newman from Montreal during the off-season about three weeks after we got Reardon. I knew nothing about Newmie, and when he reported to spring training there was no guarantee he was even going to make the team.

Funny the way things work out in this game. Newmie was in about a five-player battle for the backup infielder spot, and one of his prime competitors was Ron Gardenhire, who we had picked up from the Mets. Newmie had a little more speed, and was a little more versatile than Gardy. So Newmie made the team, and Gardy got cut.

Newmie probably cost Gardy a major-league job, but it turned out to be a good move on a couple fronts. Gardy became a minor-league coach, then a minor-league manager, and found his true calling. I think Gardy is one of the best managers in the game today. To me, he's a lot like Tom Kelly when it comes to respecting the game and emphasizing fundamentals. About the only difference is Gardy is a little more media-friendly.

Newmie became an important part of two World Series championship teams. Not only was he a very good player coming off the bench, he was one of those chemistry guys. Al always had a smile on his face, and was always happy just to be wearing a major-league uniform. He had a great sense of humor, and he turned out to be a very good friend of Kirby Puckett and Danny Gladden, the last, but certainly not the least, of the new faces added before the start of the '87 season.

Wrench

We picked up Gladden in a trade with the Giants just before breaking spring camp. The first time he came walking through the clubhouse door, I gave him the nickname "Wrench." He looked like he'd just finished doing an oil job and greasing somebody's car in the parking lot, like Mr. Goodwrench.

It's hard to know where to begin when you talk about Danny. He was a little troublemaker. He was that kid on the block who would light a fire and burn a garbage can up, and then another kid would get caught for it, and Danny would throw up his hands and say, "I had nothing to do with it."

He was a big-time instigator on a daily basis—just a ton of little things. Like he'd walk over to you in the clubhouse before a game, and say, "Geez, I heard you had a few too many cocktails last night." So you'd go find the guy you were out with and say, "Why the hell would you tell Danny I had some cocktails last night?" And of course, no one had told Danny a thing. He's just trying to stir something up. Every day he was trying to stir something up.

I think Danny was the guy who got TK thinking about giving guys a rest if there was a day game after a night game. Danny over the years got a reputation that he didn't play on Sunday. It got to be kind of a joke. You'd see Danny out on Saturday night, and you'd think he better slow down. Then you'd remember that he didn't play on Sundays.

TK learned that was a good idea pretty quick. That was the kind of thing Billy Gardner would never think of. Heck, I made all the bus trips and played every inning of every spring training game with Billy. I just didn't know anything different. I'm not sure any of us did, until Danny came along.

But Danny had a little fire to him, and I loved the way he played the game. He reminded me a lot of Johnny Castino with his drive. Danny was the kind of guy you hated playing against. He had a little cockiness about him, with that long blonde hair and a little bounce to him when he ran. He was also another guy who was a lot softer than he appeared to be. Danny was fun loving, but he was also a puppy dog at heart.

Not In Our Clubhouse

Of course, even puppy dogs get angry once in a while. And Danny had a temper, which Steve Lombardozzi can attest to. Late in the '87 season Lombo got mad about being taken out of a game, and Gladden said something to him in the clubhouse about being a man and accepting things. Well, Lombo stewed on that and ended up driving to Danny's house and knocking on the door to tell him that he was, indeed, a man. One thing led to another, and they ended up in the backyard wrestling. Danny told me that his daughters were screaming, trying to get their mom, because Daddy was fighting some guy in the yard.

Lombo ended up getting a black eye out of it. But I thought it was pretty manly of Lombo. He didn't want to bring a problem into the clubhouse, so he went and knocked on Danny's door. OK, maybe it wasn't the brightest thing to do. But give them credit: When they got back to the clubhouse the next day, you never knew anything had happened, other than Lombo had that nice shiner. A lot of guys would have had it out in the clubhouse, but that didn't happen. I'm not saying they were ever best friends, but our clubhouse was always a great place to be.

You just had to keep close tabs on your shoelaces and the shaving cream.

The Last Stand?

When we got to spring training the media focus was as much on the so-called Class of '82, as the writers dubbed the six of us who had been rookies in 1982—Gary Gaetti, Tom Brunansky, Tim Laudner, Randy Bush, Frank Viola and me—as on the off-season additions. The six of us had never done a thing as a team other than mount a brief challenge in 1984. From the start of 1982 through the 1986 season, the Twins had a record of 359-451, which isn't much to hang your hat on.

It didn't take a genius to figure out that this was a make-or-break season for us. Management had surrounded us with some talent, and if we didn't produce, the Class of '82 was going to be split up. We'd been in the league long enough that we were starting to make some decent money. Although our new owner, Carl Pohlad, had more cash than Calvin Griffith, Carl wasn't into pouring money into losing propositions.

So we heard a lot of questions that spring like, "Are you worried this is your last year together?" or "Do you feel pressure to produce this year to keep the nucleus intact?"

I guess in our hearts all of us knew it was put-up or shut-up time. We were a small market club, we'd been together for a while and it was time to win, if we were ever going to win. But honestly, other than reporters asking us about this possibly being our last year together, I never thought about it. That would be negative thinking, and like I said, my mind just doesn't work that way.

Of course, sometimes people wonder just how my mind does work.

The Snub

One of those times came when the All-Star team was picked for 1987. We were leading the AL West by two games at the break, and when they announced the AL team, we had one player—Kirby Puckett—selected as a reserve.

I've always been a guy who speaks his mind, and I felt we didn't get any respect. One pick. That's all the Twins ever got in those years, one pick. It didn't matter if you had two guys having great years, we just got one pick.

So I said I didn't want to go to any more All-Star Games. And I stuck to my guns. I played in the All-Star Game as a rookie in '82, and never went to another one. Whether me saying I didn't want to go was the reason, I don't know. And I really don't care. My goal when I started playing was not to make the All-Star team. My goal was to win the World Series.

I never saw the All-Star Game as that big of a deal. When I played, it was an ego thing to go. Now it's big money, because players get bonuses for being selected to the team. I went to one, got to swing the bat once and popped out. Big deal. It didn't mean that much to me then, and it doesn't mean much to me now.

Sure, it'd be nice to be considered an All-Star if you were picked by your peers. But as long as the fans are picking, it's off the wall. The guys who get picked are the big names who always get picked, or the guys who play in the big cities.

The File Caper

The amazing thing about winning the division in '87 was that we did it with just two quality starting pitchers: Bert Blyleven and Frank Viola. We spent most of the year trying to piece together a starting rotation, and had 12 different pitchers start games. Les Straker emerged as our No. 3 starter, although he had only an 8-10 record and 4.37 ERA.

Our front office tried just about everything to fill out the rotation, including mid-season trades that brought us veterans Joe Niekro and future Hall of Famer Steve Carlton. They were a bit past their prime, combining for a 5-14 record and a 6.39 ERA. But Joe gave us one of the season's most memorable moments during an August 3 start at California.

Most people remember the video clip: the ump, Steve Palermo, went to the mound to check out possible scuffing of the ball, and as Joe pulled out his back pocket, a file flew out. Joe ended up getting tossed out of the game and suspended for scuffing the ball.

Joe did scuff the ball, but not with a file. In fact, I could never figure out why Joe got kicked out for having a file in his pocket. Does anyone really think he pulled a file out on the mound and started sanding the ball? Of course not. But the real story never came out. Joe was scuffing the ball, but it was with a little piece of sandpaper that he had superglued to the bottom of his palm on his glove hand. No one ever knew it was there. When an ump looked at Joe's hands, he'd hold the top of his hands up, then quick flip them over and back. You could never see the little flesh-colored piece of sandpaper on his palm.

I actually knew something was up the whole game, because every time I'd catch the ball for the final out of an inning, the ump would ask for the ball. They usually don't do that, and instead let you just roll it back to the mound. Well, one inning when I got back to the dugout the first base ump was walking down the line and showed the home plate ump the ball. I went over to tell Joe, who was sitting in the runway sharpening his nails with the file. He did that between almost every inning to give him a better grip on the knuckleball that was his bread-and-butter pitch. I told him to be careful, and his response was like, "Oh, sure. OK." He wasn't going to listen to me, a kid who'd been in the league for about five years.

Joe ended up having some fun with it, going on the *David Letterman Show* wearing a belt sander. Joe was really a neat guy, and it was a shame when he died unexpectedly in 2006. To me, Joe and Steve Carlton were like grandfathers on the team. I went out for dinner with the two of them one night in Detroit, and the chance to listen to their stories and talk baseball was something I'll never forget.

Puck's Big Weekend

The season itself was a rollercoaster. We had a great home record, but for some reason we couldn't seem to win on the road. We had a five-game lead over Oakland in mid-August. Then we went on the road and lost six straight at Detroit and Boston. On the night of August 28, we'd lost nine of 10 games and were in a virtual tie with the A's for first place (66-62 for Oakland, 67-63 for us).

The next two games at Milwaukee belonged to Kirby Puckett. We beat the Brewers 12-3 and then 10-6. Puck was 10-for-11 with seven runs scored and six RBIs. He was 6-for-6 in the second game.

By the time we left Milwaukee we had a one-game lead that we never relinquished. A lot of people point to Puck's weekend as the key point of the season. It was certainly one of the key points, and one of the greatest hitting weekends I've seen. But I have a hard time pointing to any one thing as a key in '87, because that was a team with an incredible amount of unsung heroes.

Our middle infield combination of Steve Lombardozzi and Greg Gagne never received much credit, but they were as

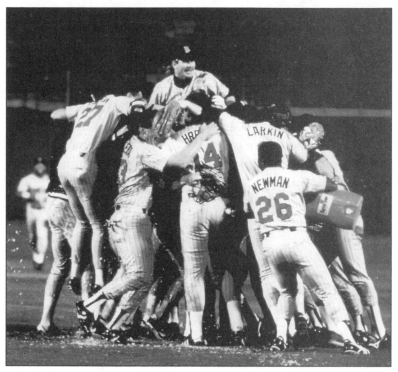

We went crazy when we clinched the AL West Division title in Texas in 1987. Courtesy of the Minnesota Twins

important as anybody. This will surprise some people, but to me Lombo was the best second baseman I ever played with. He was better defensively than Chuck Knoblauch, I think. Gags was a better shortstop than a lot of people think, but he never got any recognition.

Well, I shouldn't say that. Gags got attention every time our training staff would do the body fat tests. I used to say that Gags had this chicken skin. You could take his skin and just pull it out until you could hardly believe how far it came. He used to measure about four. I always had the highest, about 19. No one told me the low score won. But that was always Gags, with that chicken skin, the thick eastern accent and the smile with those big old teeth of his.

There wasn't a better player than Puck on the team, and that weekend was unforgettable, but that weekend didn't win us the division. It's almost fitting that Lombo broke a 3-3 tie with an eighth-inning single the night we clinched the division with 5-3 win at Texas. Lombo had a ton of big hits down the stretch.

We won it as a team of 25 guys. Twenty-five guys who loved to burn shoelaces and put shaving cream in telephones. That's what made us what we were in 1987.

CHAPTER ELEVEN

The Postseason

After we beat Texas, we sprayed champagne and beer for the first time as major leaguers. And then we promptly went out and lost the final five games of the regular season, which had people wondering about the importance of momentum in the postseason. The answer: no importance whatsoever. All we proved down the stretch was that it's tough to play with a hangover.

Most people overlooked us at the start of postseason because of our record. But that record was largely due to our inability to fill out a five-man rotation. When we got into the playoffs, we had Bert Blyleven and Frank Viola as our one-two punch, with Les Straker as No. 3. Because we didn't need a No. 4 or 5, we were a much better postseason team than we were during the regular season.

We showed it immediately, beating the Tigers two straight at home. Gary Gaetti hit a pair of homers in the first game, and we rallied from a 5-4 deficit with four runs in the bottom of the eighth to win 8-5. In the second game, I homered off Jack Morris in the fifth inning, which helped Bert Blyleven pitch us to a 6-3 victory.

We learned those two games that we were going to have one of the greatest postseason home-field advantages in baseball history. I can still remember the feeling I had walking downstairs to go onto the field for Game 1 of the playoffs. The place was electric. And once the game started, the noise was so incredible it made the hair stand up on the back of your neck. I was so jacked up to play in that atmosphere that I didn't even feel like my feet were touching the ground when I ran out to first to start the game. I had never heard anything like the noise in the Dome those first two games, and I'm not sure anyone else in baseball ever had, either.

True to our regular-season form, we went to Detroit for Game 3 and promptly lost 7-6 when Pat Sheridan hit a two-run homer off Jeff Reardon in the bottom of the eighth. Reardon showed me something after that game when he walked out of the trainer's room to talk with reporters. He could have sat in there icing his arm and blown everybody off. But Term was a stand-up guy.

All year Tom Kelly had been telling us to take it one game at a time, don't get too hung up on worrying about the future. That became ingrained in us, and when we lost Game 3, it was just one game. Don't get too high, don't get too low—that was another one of his sayings. We came back and won Game 4 behind Frank Viola 5-3, and took the series with Blyleven beating the Tigers 9-5 in Game 5.

The Homecoming

After we celebrated in the Tiger Stadium clubhouse, we got on a charter and headed back to Minnesota. They announced on the flight back that there was going to be a little celebration at the Dome, and they wanted us to bus down there. I'll be honest: None of us were too excited when we heard about it. We were all tired, and we wanted nothing more than to get in our cars and go home and get some rest before the World Series. But it was mandatory, so what are you going to do?

The first estimate we heard on the flight was that 5,000 people might be there. By the time we landed they said traffic was building around the Dome, and there might be 10,000 people, maybe even 15,000. By the time we were onboard the bus to the Dome they told us there would be 20,000 people. The ride from the airport to the Dome is about 10 miles, and by the time we were halfway there, there was already traffic congestion. We looked around at each other and couldn't quite figure out what was going on, but we were starting to get a pretty good idea.

They ended up sending a police escort out to meet us, which was a good thing because the traffic around the Dome was crazy. There were people jamming the sidewalks as we pulled into the back loading dock of the Dome. That allowed us to go in the back security entrance, and enter the field together through a huge door in the back of the Dome that looked like a giant garage door. The door opened up, and I don't think any of us were prepared for what we saw.

That whole building was packed. And we heard there were more people out on the sidewalk who couldn't even get in. We walked in and the stands were a blue haze—I don't think anyone was monitoring the no-smoking ban in the Dome—with Homer Hankies everywhere. We looked at each other in amazement, all of us thinking the same thing: "What the hell is going on here?" We got out on the field, and I looked over at G-Man and he was balling his eyes out. A bunch of guys had tears in their eyes. It was kind of an ad-lib night, with a few speeches, but mostly fans cheering and us waving. Joe Niekro flipped open his back pocket and a file flew out. At least he wasn't wearing his belt sander, although had he been given the chance to swing by his home he probably would have.

There are a lot of guys on the team who rate that as one of the most special memories of the entire season, including the World Series. We had more than 50,000 people show up for an impromptu nighttime celebration. I'm not sure you'll ever see anything like that again. We were kind of like a small town experiencing something for the first time. It's probably what it's like in a little northern Minnesota town when the high school is going to its first state hockey tournament.

I think part of what made it special was that Twins fans had watched the core of our team grow up together. They'd watched us lose 102 games as rookies, and watched us lose a whole lot more games than we won over the next four seasons. We literally grew up before our fans' eyes. And I think there was a special bond that two of the starters—Timmy Laudner and myself—were native Minnesotans. If you live in New York or Chicago you probably wouldn't understand that. But we're a little provincial, a little small town, in stuff like that. There's nothing like being "one of us."

The other part that made it special was that we had a chance to be a part of Minnesota sports history. Minnesota had been to the 1965 World Series and lost to the Dodgers, but hadn't been back since. The old Minneapolis Lakers had won a bunch of NBA titles in the 1950s, but that was before the NBA became big-time. The Vikings had lost four Super Bowls under Bud Grant. Minnesota sports fans were starting to develop an inferiority complex. We had a chance to be the first Minnesota team to ever win a major sports championship. And our fans were ready.

Prelude to a Grand Slam

I can condense the first five games of the World Series against St. Louis pretty quickly: We won the first two at home, then went to St. Louis and got swept in three games—the typical pattern for us: Win at home, lose on the road.

Games 6 and 7 of the Series were so memorable that the first five games were pretty much overshadowed. That was certainly the case for me. I didn't do much at the plate, but then I didn't do much against the Tigers in the American League playoffs, either. I was 3-for-20 against Detroit, and 4-for-17 in the first five games against the Cardinals, which left me on the wrong side of .200 for the postseason.

I can't say we felt a real sense of urgency coming back to the Dome for Games 6 and 7. That might sound a little dumb, because we knew if we lost one more game, we were done. But we were coming home to the building where we'd played so well all year, and we just had a confidence that things were going to be OK.

Having said that, I think most people still figured we were the underdog. We had Les Straker starting in Game 6. Les was a 28-year-old rookie who had never pitched in a setting like this. Not only that, the day before his start he told reporters that he had never started on three days' rest as a professional, and that his right elbow was hurting. That angered Tom Kelly, who had a pregame shouting match with the local reporter who wrote the Straker story. It didn't help when the reporter told Kelly that the same story had appeared in every major daily in America. TK wasn't overly fond of a lot of local media, and a lot of the local media felt the same way about him. It was a tenuous relationship at best, and this time TK felt he'd been made to look bad. Turned out the reports on Straker were pretty accurate. Les lasted three innings, and we were down 5-2 entering the bottom of the fifth.

But all year it seemed like if we needed a two-run homer, someone would step up and hit a two-run homer. This time it was Don Baylor, who we picked up in late August to give us a right-handed power hitter off the bench. Don hadn't hit a home run as a Twin until he hit a two-run shot in the fifth to tie the game. A couple hitters later Steve Lombardozzi singled in the go-ahead run for a 6-5 lead.

The Grand Slam

We had a chance to take control of the game in the bottom of the sixth when we loaded the bases with one out. But Tom Brunansky popped out against Bob Forsch for the second out. The Cardinals brought in veteran lefty Ken Dayley to face me.

I hadn't been hitting for crap the whole postseason. When you're struggling like that, Randy Bush would always tell people to swing hard, just in case you hit it. But when I looked toward the dugout at the plate against Dayley, Kelly was making an "S" sign across his chest. Everyone knew what that meant: Don't try to be Superman. Just get the bat on the ball.

That's probably as much as anyone was hoping for, since I was 1-for-14 in the Series against lefties as I came to the plate to face Dayley. As I stepped into the batter's box, I told myself that if the first pitch was a strike, I was swinging. It was, and I did.

Dayley threw me a fastball, and I was lucky enough to get my bat on the ball and hit it 439 feet over the center-field fence for a grand-slam home run. That was by far the biggest home run I ever hit.

I still think it might have been one of the most special home runs anyone ever hit, for the simple reason that I hit it playing for the Minnesota Twins. That at-bat was what I'd dreamed of since I was a little kid. I hit that home run a million times for the Twins in my backyard playing wiffle ball. And now I had done it for real, for the team I grew up watching. There aren't a lot of stories like that.

I still have people stop me and tell me what they were doing the night I hit that grand slam. One guy told me he was at his wedding reception, and I pretty much put a stop to the wedding dance because everyone was gathered around a TV in the bar and the whole place went nuts. Another guy told me he was out driving his tractor in South Dakota and can still

My grand slam in Game 6 gave us the momentum we needed to beat the Cardinals. Courtesy of the Minnesota Twins

remember standing up and cheering. Things like that I still get all the time.

That home run gave us the momentum, and we went on to an 11-5 victory and a showdown Game 7.

To this day, people stop me on the street to tell me where they were when I hit my Game 6 grand slam. Courtesy of the Minnesota Twins

After the Slam

My buddy, Wade Boelter was at Game 6, and he and his wife, Natalie, and Jeanie and I went out after the game. I've known Wade since junior high, and we were the best man at each other's wedding. And now he and his wife live down the block from us. We left the Dome about 7:30 that night and stopped for dinner at Fletcher's on Lake Minnetonka. Jeanie and I ate at Fletcher's quite a bit, because I was still living on the lake at the time.

I had my standard fare—prime rib—and we ordered a bottle of champagne. I thought I deserved a glass of champagne after the grand slam. Jeanie saved the cork from that bottle, and we still have it downstairs, with Game 6 written on it as a reminder of the night.

I'd been to the restaurant enough that having Kent Hrbek eating dinner there was no big deal. It was exciting, but fairly subdued, although a few people came up and high-fived me. Minneapolis back then was the kind of place you could hit a World Series grand slam and still go out and have a nice meal without getting mauled. The people were polite and let us eat in relative peace. But you could sense the anticipation of Game 7.

We got home about 10 and my phone rang. It was Wade's cousin from Litchfield, which is about 50 to 60 miles west of the Twin Cities. Wade's cousins were the Piepenberg brothers—Dale, Kevin and Doug—and I'd been hunting with them and their dad, Bud, a bunch of times. I could hear Wade saying, "Ah, you're nuts. He's not going with us tomorrow."

I said, "What's going on?" Wade put his hand over the phone and said the Bluebills came in last night. Well, when the Bluebills come in, you've usually got a two- or three-day hunt, and that's it. The ducks are in, then they're out. So I said to Wade: "Let's go." And Wade turned to me and said, "We're not going. You've got a fairly important ball game tomorrow," meaning Game 7 of the World Series.

I told Wade I wasn't going to be able to sleep all night anyway, so I'd go to bed early, get a couple hours of sleep, be hunting by sunrise and come home and take a nap. That's nothing I wouldn't have done on a normal game day. I used to get up early and go fishing a lot, contrary to what my former manager Ray Miller might have thought.

So Wade finally relented, and said if you want to go, we'll go. Jeanie was always great about making sure I stayed on the right path and didn't do too many goofy things. I don't remember her saying, "No, you idiot, you're not going."

Wade and his wife stayed overnight at our house, and we got up and left about 5 a.m. the next morning. I drove my pickup to Litchfield, and as was often the case I was low on gas. So we pulled into a station in Hutchinson, about 35 miles west of Minneapolis, and I asked Wade to pump the gas and go inside to pay because if I walked in they were going to ask: "What the hell is Kent Hrbek doing out here at 5:30 the morning of Game 7?" I actually wasn't all that concerned about that—getting Wade to go in was just a ploy to get him to pay for the gas.

It worked. Wade went in, paid and came back with this big shit-eating grin on his face. He said the morning paper was out already, and my mug was plastered all over the front page. Wade said when he walked in, there was a group of guys talking about the Twins, and a highway patrol guy turned to him and said, "You think the boys are going to do it tonight?" Wade told me he came this close to telling the trooper, "Why don't you just go ask the guy sitting in the truck?" But he bit his tongue.

When we reached the slew, I realized I must have been a little distracted. A flock flew over, and I'd forgotten to put bullets in my gun. I was probably thinking about the game, at least subconsciously. But in the end, we got some ducks, drove home and I took a nice little nap and then headed to the ballpark.

To me, it was no big deal. I'm not the kind of person who's going to sit and dwell on something. I'm going to do it my way, and for the most part that's worked for me. I'm pretty certain of this: I got more sleep that night, counting my nap, than our Game 7 starter, Frank Viola. Knowing Frankie, he was definitely up all night.

Game 7

The way I looked at it, getting a chance to play in the deciding game of the World Series was fun. Sure, as we got ready in the clubhouse you could sense there were pressure and some butterflies. You sure didn't want to be the one who screwed up in that setting. But this was the ultimate—the reason you played the game.

As I got ready, my mind went back to John Castino and Gary Ward the day I walked in to Yankee Stadium in 1981 as a 21-year-old rookie. This was the same game I'd been playing since I was a little kid—whether it was in my backyard, Yankee Stadium or the Metrodome for Game 7.

As I look back on the game, it was almost like we expected to win. We'd won our big games at home all year, and after getting past Game 6 we came back for the final game with one of our two aces, Frank Viola, on the mound. Of course, in any sport, once you start thinking you're going to win, you're in trouble. You've got to keep that sort of thinking out of your head, and go out and play hard. I'm just saying as I look back, in hindsight, it seemed like we were destined to win.

We did, but it wasn't easy. We fell behind 2-0 in the top of the second and clawed our way back, scoring single runs in four separate innings. Our go-ahead run—and the eventual game-winner—came in the bottom of the sixth when Greg Gagne beat out an infield single with the bases loaded.

Once we got the lead, Frankie and Jeff Reardon closed the door. They were superb. Frank went eight innings, gave up six hits, didn't walk a batter and struck out seven. Jeff slammed the door shut in the ninth, and I had the everlasting memory of catching the throw from Gary Gaetti for the final out. I've heard

My teammates mob me after I caught the throw from Gary Gaetti for the final out of the World Series. Courtesy of the Minnesota Twins

guys from that team talk about the homecoming after beating the Tigers as the emotional memory from the postseason. But for me, nothing compared to catching that throw for the final out.

Time For a Laugh

We played our final game in typical fashion, meaning we looked for any chance we could to play a practical joke. We were trailing 2-1 after the top of the fifth inning. Bob Casey, the public address announcer, used the break between innings to use the bathroom, requiring him to run from his little area under the stands directly behind the backstop to a tiny bathroom just off our dugout. Casey is a legendary figure in Twins history—the public address voice for every Twins game from the time the team moved to Minnesota in 1961 until his death in 2005. Casey was a true character, which made him a target for pranks.

So, in the seventh game of the Series, we did what we usually did, which was hold the door and make him think he was locked in. I think it was Tom Brunansky who held the door, and while he was doing that someone ran into Casey's PA area and put shaving cream in his telephone earpiece and soaked a towel in shaving cream, so that when he wiped off his ear he'd end up with even more shaving cream on his face.

The plan worked to perfection. We'd always release Casey from the bathroom so he could make it back in time for the first pitch. Bruno waited long enough that Casey was hopping mad, screaming at us as he raced to get to his microphone. We waited a couple minutes, then placed an emergency call to the PA phone. Casey grabbed the phone and his ear ended up soaked in shaving cream. He grabbed the towel, and ended up getting shaving cream all over his suit as he tried to wipe his ear off. We were howling in the dugout as we watched all this go on.

That was one of the best shaving cream stunts of the whole season. A few years later Casey remembered it like this: "All I heard was laughter. Those dummies didn't know they were in the seventh game of the World Series." He might have been right.

Bruno also had the other memorable joke of the World Series. He saw a fake nail-through-the-hand gadget at some joke store, and during an off-day workout took it out to the outfield with some ketchup and a white towel. Near the end of the workout he came running off the field, his hand wrapped in a ketchup-soaked towel with a nail appearing to have pierced his hand.

He was screaming about the damn outfield fence, that he had jammed his hand into a loose nail. The media started running around, thinking there was a breaking news story about the Twins losing their starting right fielder to a fluke accident. Bruno let it go on for a few minutes, then pulled the fake nail out of his

I gave owner Carl Pohlad a huge hug right after we won the world championship. Courtesy of the Minnesota Twins

hand and everyone had a good laugh, except for a few media members who might have filed an emergency news flash.

That was our team in '87—loose and fun. We had a 10-year reunion in 1997, and our general manager, Andy MacPhail, said that fifth-inning intermission of Game 7 was his defining memory of the season. "I'm so nervous I can hardly watch the game, much less participate in it, and they're thinking about locking Casey in the bathroom," he told a reporter during the reunion. "To me, that's the memory that will forever highlight that group."

I think that's the way all of us will remember that team. We took a lot of pride in being called "throwbacks." We had something real unique. I'm not sure there has been a World Series winner since that had more fun, or more characters, than we did in '87. Baseball started becoming more and more of a business after that, and I think the business part started to become bigger than the game part.

The guys who left the Twins in the years that followed found out just how unique we were that year. Brunansky said he just naturally assumed all teams had fun and enjoyed the game and each other the way he did. But when he was traded, he found out otherwise.

The Aftermath

After the game we had another beer and champagne celebration in the clubhouse. By now we were getting used to that. What I remember most from the clubhouse after the game was sitting on the floor when my buddy Wade walked in. He said, "Man, are you drunk already?" I might have looked that way, because I was sitting on the floor smoking a cigar.

But I wasn't drunk at all. I was totally exhausted. I don't think any of us had any idea how tired we were—how pumped up we were on adrenaline—until after the game, when you can finally take a breath and say that it's over. I don't think any of us had been sleeping a whole lot, and we were much more consumed by the entire experience than we even thought.

It's funny, but having grown up a Twins fan I wanted to be outside the Dome, celebrating in the streets with the fans. At one point, while we still had our uniforms on, I asked Danny Gladden if he wanted to go outside and celebrate with the fans. Danny displayed unusual common sense for him, and said, "What are you, crazy? They'll tear our uniforms off and kill us."

So we stayed in the clubhouse and celebrated a while with our wives, families, and friends. You'll never guess where I ended up that night: the Perkins Restaurant off France and Interstate 494 in Bloomington with my family. My plan was to end the night by taking a bottle of champagne and sit on the pitching mound at Bloomington Kennedy High School. That seemed kind of fitting, because that was where it had all started for me. But I never made it. I was so pooped I just went home after Perkins.

The Parade

The biggest celebration came a couple days later when the cities of Minneapolis and St. Paul threw us a ticker-tape parade. I still can't believe it when I look at the photos from the parade. We all rode in convertibles, and all along the route there were thousands of fans jammed so close to the cars that we had trouble even moving. There was so much ticker tape thrown into the cars that the one Sal Butera was riding in had a small fire on the floor.

Jeanie and I shared a car with our equipment manager, Jimmy Wiesner, and his wife, Marge. That was a fantasy fulfilled for both of us. Wiesey grew up in Minnesota like me, and had always dreamed of winning a World Series with the Twins.

There are some organizations where the equipment manager maybe wouldn't have even ridden in the parade, or would have been stuck in a car in the back. Wiesey and I had talked for several years about riding together in the same car if the Twins

During the ticker-tape parade the Twin Cities held for us, I was honored to ride in the same car as equipment manager Jimmy Wiesner, his wife, Marge, and my wife, Jeanie. Courtesy of the Minnesota Twins

ever won a World Series. Some of that goes back to the way I feel about what it takes to have a winning ballclub. If you're going to win a World Series, then you've got everyone, from the batboys to the players to the front office, all on the same page. You're all one team, and you should all be treated like you're important parts of the team.

Most of the reason I wanted to ride with Wiesey, though, was knowing how much winning meant to him, and the respect I had for him. Wiesey was a huge part of the team. The guy spent 16 hours a day downstairs in the clubhouse, and he kept it as clean as his own home. There were clubhouse managers in the majors who had a lot better facilities to work with, but no one did a better job than Wiesey. Our clubhouse was always a comfortable place to be.

I will never forget the huge and happy crowds that welcomed us home during the ticker-tape parade. The fans were wall to wall. What an experience! Courtesy of the Minnesota Twins

Jimmy and I have cried more than once as we've talked together, reminiscing about the parade. The parade kind of put a stamp on the whole postseason experience. Everything about that October was so spontaneous. You couldn't go anywhere in the Twin Cities without seeing banners or signs or garage doors painted with "Go Twins."

My wife taped some of the news shows after we won, and when I went back and watched them, even I was surprised by how much it meant to people. There was one news clip in particular, where they interviewed some guy who had been working in the same warehouse for 46 years. He said that the Series had been the most fun he'd ever had going to work, because everybody was talking about the same thing, and everybody was happy. He said he'd never been so happy to come to work.

That's pretty special, to know you had made so many people so happy. It was electrifying, like the entire state was into it. I don't think Minnesota—and the Upper Midwest as a whole—has been able to duplicate what happened that October. And I'm not sure it ever will.

CHAPTER TWELVE

The Slide

Go Figure

One of the most mystifying events I've ever been associated with took place on April 22, 1988. That's the day we traded Tom Brunansky to the Cardinals for Tom Herr. Twenty years later I still don't get it.

Yes, we got off to a rough start in '88 (4-10 at the time of the deal). But we were less than three weeks into the season, and virtually the same team had been good enough to win a world championship the previous summer. I don't think anybody on our team ever understood it. It sure wasn't like Bruno was a cancer we needed to get out of the clubhouse. Bruno was a peach, an absolutely great guy.

I guess our general manager, Andy MacPhail, always liked Herr and thought his left-handed power would be perfect for the Dome, with its short right-field fence. I guess Andy also must have thought we needed to be shaken up after that slow start.

He accomplished that. We were all just shocked. For me, it was the first guy from our Class of '82 rookie group—Bruno, Gary Gaetti, Randy Bush, Tim Laudner, Frank Viola and me—

When the Twins traded my buddy Tom Brunansky in 1988, I was shocked, but I still tried to have fun on the field. Courtesy of the Minnesota Twins

to be traded. We'd been through so much together, and after all that, Bruno was gone.

What can you do? Andy made a lot of great trades. This just wasn't one of them. At the time it was numbing, and all you can do is go out and do your job. And my job was to play first base and bat cleanup for the Twins. I didn't get paid to make trades, or comment on them. One thing I've never understood are players who feel they should have a say in what the front office does.

Torii Hunter did that a couple years ago, saying he should have been contacted about a move the team made. I have a lot of respect for Torii, but I've never understood that logic. A player has a job to do, and he needs to go out and do it to the best of his ability and not get caught up in other stuff. That's the attitude I took when Bruno was traded, even though it wasn't easy.

Herr's Reaction

The trade got more difficult to accept when Herr arrived the next day, and we learned he'd been crying on the flight to Minneapolis. Now, I'm not going to hold that against him. He probably felt as bad leaving the Cardinals as we felt about losing Bruno.

But he never got over it. I think we—and I mean as a team— could have gotten over the trade if Herr had gotten over his personal disappointment. But I don't think he ever wanted to be here, and it showed. I don't think Tom Kelly was too happy with his attitude, because he just didn't fit in with our clubhouse. As I said earlier, he's the only teammate I ever had that I didn't care for. And it had everything to do with his attitude, or lack thereof.

Still, we rebounded and played some pretty good baseball that summer, winning 91 games, which was more than we'd won in '87. But it wasn't enough because the Oakland A's—the Bash Brothers—won 104 games.

If you look back, the Bruno trade was the beginning of the end for our '87 team. Much of the rest of the nucleus was gone in short order. Before the start of the 1989 season, the Twins traded Bert Blyleven, Steve Lombardozzi, and Keith Atherton. Oh, yeah…we dumped Herr on the Phillies in a trade for left-hander Shane Rawley less than a month after the 1988 season ended.

It was the end of an era—in a lot of ways.

No. 400

I absolutely hated to see Blyleven go, because we had ridden Bert and Frank Viola to a World Series title in '87. And now half that tandem was gone. I knew what it was like without strong starting pitching, and I feared we could be headed there again. And I was right.

We had losing records in both 1989 and '90. By the end of the '90 season, I felt like I was back where I had started in my Twins career, playing on a club that was sifting through pitchers looking for starters. In 1988, we had three pitchers—Blyleven, Frank Viola, and Alan Anderson—throw more than 200 innings. The next two years, no one threw that many. The days of riding pitching horses to the top were over.

Not that losing Bert was all bad. Bert had one of the nastiest curveballs I'd ever seen, and a better-than-average fastball. Yet for some reason, I owned him. I was always able to hit Bert, and he knew it. After he left the Twins and went to California, Bert gave up career home run No. 400 against me. Someone took a picture of me at the plate and gave it to Bert. The next day he sent it over to our clubhouse in a frame, with this inscription: "Thanks for No. 400. Maybe you'll be the guy to hit No. 500. Then again, you fat pig, you probably won't be around then."

Bert knew me pretty well, didn't he? I watched Bert pitch with the Twins when I was a kid, and I felt fortunate to have had the chance to play with him. He was one of the guys who gave you everything he had. He always gave up a lot of homers, but if you check you'll find most of them were solo homers that didn't hurt him.

My lasting memory of Bert might be more smell than anything else. Our trainer, Dick Martin, used to rub the hottest atomic balm on Bert's back and shoulder the day he pitched. I couldn't even put my finger in the stuff, because it burned. There were three different kinds of balm in our trainer's room, but until Bert showed up, no one ever used the atomic hot stuff. Dick had to put on rubber gloves to rub the stuff on Bert's shoulder.

Bert had enough innings on that right shoulder that he needed the super hot stuff to loosen up the muscles. He was a true workhouse.

Little Big Man

The unfortunate trade for Herr put the handwriting on the wall for Lombardozzi. Lombo stuck around through the '88 season, then was traded to Houston near the end of the 1989 spring training.

The strange thing is, the relationship between Lombo and Tom Kelly might have been one of the big reasons the trade for Herr was made in the first place. I think maybe TK wanted to find a second baseman to move Lombo out, and we ended up with Herr. Talk about backfiring. TK and Lombo just weren't on the same page, and TK wasn't the kind of manager to tolerate players who weren't on his page.

I think Lombo had a little bit of what they call "Little Big Man Disease." Lombo went to the University of Florida, and he was probably a big stud in college. TK was big on fundamentals and doing all the little things that make teams winners. Well, Lombo wanted to be more than a guy who advanced people over, and get hit-and-run signs. He wanted to be The Guy once in a while. That's how I saw the rift develop between TK and Lombo.

Lombo would get frustrated when he was given a bunt sign, and he showed that frustration. And I think that really pissed TK off.

Probably the final straw came in the '87 World Series. Lombo had a great World Series (7-for-17, four RBIs). After the Cardinals jumped to a 2-0 lead in Game 7, Lombo had a two-out RBI single in the bottom of the second to score our first run. At that point, Lombo looked like one of the leading contenders to be the World Series MVP. And he might have won it with one more big hit, but he never got the chance. In the bottom of the sixth with the score tied 2-2, and two runners on and one out, TK pinch hit Roy Smalley for Lombo.

The move made strategic sense, because the Cardinals had right-hander Todd Worrell pitching, and Smalley was a switch-hitter, while Lombo was a right-handed hitter. But Lombo didn't see it that way, of course. I didn't see it, but I'm told Lombo stormed up the runway and threw his helmet when TK told him he was going to send up Smalley as a pinch-hitter. You can guess how that went over with TK in Game 7 of the World Series.

For the record, the move worked. Smalley walked to load the bases with one out. Dan Gladden struck out, but Greg Gagne beat out an infield single with two out that scored Bruno with what proved to be the winning run in a 4-2 victory.

The sad thing is, the rift ended up hurting both TK and Lombo. We got saddled with Tom Herr, and Lombo ended up getting traded to Houston. Lombo never got a chance to start in Houston, and he was out of the majors at the end of the 1990 season. I know Lombo always felt he got labeled with a bad attitude. Like I said, Lombo was the best defensive second baseman I ever played with, and he had a little pop in his bat, too.

You take a look at the careers of Lombo and Herr, and you realize baseball is a strange game. Sometimes it has as much to do with personalities as performance.

More Changes

Our slide really started in 1989, and years like that I've pretty much forgotten about—at least the games. You remember the people. Another Class of '82 member, Tim Laudner, played his final game in 1989.

Tim played most of his major-league career with a sore right knee, and finally had surgery in early September of '89. He tried to come back the next spring, but ended up leaving the club and never played in another big-league game. Timmy and I had been high school rivals and were both called up to the majors for the first time late in the 1981 season. It's hard to see guys like that leave the team. Timmy's remained in the Twin Cities, and we still see each other from time to time.

It's kind of funny looking back, but my number through high school was always 15. When I got called up to the big leagues in 1981, I had jersey No. 26 hanging in my locker, and I was just so happy to be there I didn't give the number any thought. You wore whatever number they gave you in the minors, and I think I had No. 29 at Visalia that summer.

Timmy got called up about two days after me, and when he walked into the clubhouse he had No. 15 hanging in his locker. It was kind of funny, because that used to be my number and had I thought of it, I'm sure I could have requested it. But I never said anything, and when I showed up for spring training the next year, I had No. 14 hanging in my locker. I have no idea why they made the change, and at the time it was no big deal. But over the years I grew pretty attached to No. 14.

Frank's Farewell

The most memorable thing about the summer of '89 was the departure of another Class of '82 guy, Frank Viola, right before the July trading deadline.

A lot of people were under the impression that Frank and I had a falling out and didn't get along. That wasn't really the case. I did get upset with Frank that summer when he made a statement to the effect that he thought a trade might be a good thing for him. I just told Frank that if he didn't want to pitch here anymore, then no one wanted him around. I don't think that was really a rift. That's just the way I'd feel about any teammate. If you go public that you don't want to be here, then it was time to leave.

It was a rough year, mostly because of pitching. Our offensive stats were pretty comparable to what they'd been in 1987, but in '89, we had no Bert Blyleven to lead the way. Frankie and Alan Anderson were about all we had in the way of starting pitching.

Andy MacPhail clearly realized that, too. Frank, after winning the Cy Young in 1988, was pretty attractive trade bait. Andy was able to get five pitchers from the Mets for Frank: Rick Aguilera, Kevin Tapani, David West, Jack Savage and Tim Drummond. Five-for-one. The odds are one or two of them are going to work out, and that's what happened for us. Aggie became one of the best relievers in the league, and Tap became a solid starting pitcher.

I wasn't sad to see Frank go. He wanted out, and hopefully he was moving on to bigger and better things. Frankie was a different guy—one of the most nervous guys I'd ever been around. On the days he pitched, he had to take anti-diarrhea medicine so he wouldn't crap his pants on the mound. I'm sure that'll surprise people, because he looked so in control on the mound. But inside he was as nervous as a whore in church when it was his day to pitch.

My relationship with Frankie was a little like my relationship with Kirby Puckett. I thought they were both great players and great teammates. But I didn't hang around with either one of them away from the ballpark. That's just the way it is on a team. They had guys they were close to, I had guys I was close to.

But if I had to rank my favorite starting pitchers to play behind, Frank would be in the top four. I'd put Bert and Jack Morris at the top, tied for one, followed by Frankie and Kevin Tapani. No one knows about Tap. But he was just like the others on that list: When he got the ball back from the catcher, he didn't waste any time. And he threw strikes. Those are the guys you want to be playing behind. They were competitors, they worked fast and they threw strikes.

Am I Gone?

My contract expired after the 1989 season, and for most players that would have been the end of their Twins career. They'd have taken the money and run to a bigger market and brighter lights. I had the chance.

Detroit, Seattle, and Boston all offered more money. I could have gotten $15.5 million for five years if I'd have left the Twins. But I took $14 million for five years to stay with Minnesota. For a while it didn't look like the Twins were even going to be in the neighborhood of the other offers, and that might have forced my hand to move on.

There was one night that Jeanie and I sat downstairs, in what I call the Twins room because she's decorated it with all the memorabilia from my career. We talked seriously that night about the possibility of leaving. We sat at the counter, surrounded by Twins stuff everywhere, and talked about whether it was worth moving. In the end, we just couldn't see ourselves doing that. Our roots run too deep in Minnesota, and I didn't want to dig them up. But then again, I wasn't going to stay in Minnesota for half the money that others were offering.

I called my agent, Ron Simon, and told him that if he could get the Twins to make a competitive offer, I wanted to stay in Minnesota. Ron's a native Minnesotan, and he understood how I felt. We had to play the game out, and threaten to leave, but we both knew that wasn't what Jeanie and I wanted.

In the end, what's a couple million dollars over five years? Am I going to be happier trying to spend $15.5 million than I am $14 million? So that was Ron's goal, to try to get the Twins within a couple million dollars.

That off-season made me think a lot about players who had to move around during their careers. Think about how tough that is—to pack up your family and move, find a new home, go to new schools. You follow the money, and that's what you get.

Bowling For Dollars

It was a Wednesday afternoon when I got the call from Ron that the Twins had hit our figure. Being Wednesday meant I was bowling in a league at the West Side Lanes in South St. Paul. It was kind of nice to get the news there, because that Wednesday league has been a staple of the Twins organization for years, and I was surrounded by friends when I got the news. It helped balance out the other news of the day: Earlier that morning Jeff Reardon announced that he was going to sign with the Red Sox.

But everyone was happy when I told them my news, and I got a lot of slaps on the back and probably a few more beers bought for me. That league is one of the neat things about being a Twin. I don't think many other organizations have an off-season weekly get-together like that.

Billy Martin and Tony Oliva bowled in it in the early '60s, with a bunch of front-office people like Don Cassidy and Jim Rantz. When I played, we had Ron Davis, Kirby Puckett, Gene Larkin, Al Newman and Gary Gaetti. There were others, too, who'd show up to sub when we needed someone. Ron Gardenhire, pitching coach Rick Anderson and I still bowl in the league every Wednesday.

I've met some of my best friends in that league. The average age of the guys in the league is about 70, and we had a guy sub for us, Frank Kulhanek, who was 94 years old and wasn't afraid to stick around after bowling to have a beer with us.

Bowling and beer—it doesn't get much better than that. I spent a lot of time as a kid at bowling alleys, because my mom and dad were both bowlers. Over the years, I developed a real fondness for the game.

In fact, I consider bowling to be one of the greatest sports in the world. You can sit and drink a beer, get up and throw a ball and it comes right back to you. You don't have to chase it or anything.

How great is that?

Costly Prank

The joy over my new contract didn't last long. We hit rock bottom in 1990, finishing last in the AL West, so far behind the A's all we could see was their dust. Hard to believe that a couple years earlier we had been the A's chief rival. I think all the changes just caught up to us. We were in a rebuilding mode, trying to work Rick Aguilera in as a closer and find a starting rotation.

I had a solid year, although my power numbers (22 homers, 79 RBIs) would have been better had I not missed the final two weeks with a fractured ankle. Now, I'd like to end the story there, and let you think I did it sliding into second base to break up a double play. Something with a little guts and glory to it.

The truth is I broke my ankle chasing one of the clubhouse attendants in the clubhouse lunchroom. I was sitting at a table talking with one of our clubhouse guys, Chico McGinn, and a couple other people. Another clubhouse guy, Jimmy Dunn, was working the visitors' room at the time. We called Jimmy "Doughboy," because he looked a little like the Pillsbury Doughboy. I'd been ragging on Doughboy about something, and he came around the corner and flipped me off. So I jumped up and was going to try to catch him.

As soon as I rounded the first corner, my ankle cracked. I went down, and a bunch of guys just stood there, thinking I was screwing around. I wasn't. After I got to my feet I knew something was really wrong, and I told Chico to go tell TK that I wasn't going to make it out for pregame. Chico looked at me and said, "No way. I'm not telling TK."

So I did it myself. TK wasn't too happy with me, but he knew that was just me being myself. I always joked around with the clubhouse guys. I didn't walk around on glass worried about getting hurt. We used to wrestle and chase each other all the time. This time I just happened to get hurt.

I think that's the only time I ever got hurt screwing around. I did end up with a bent finger once, and it's still bent to this day. That came when we were shagging balls in the outfield in Cleveland before a game, trying to make goofy catches. I had my glove on, but it caught me right on the tip of my finger, I thought I broke it, but I was able to tape it up and play.

I wasn't so lucky chasing Doughboy. The thing about that is I was honest about it with everyone, including the media. I know that a lot of guys get injured off the field, and the media gets told it happened the night before sliding into second, or whatever. A lot of injuries that happen off the field get hidden from the media. But I didn't do that. And I wasn't ashamed to say I got hurt screwing around in the clubhouse. You've got to have fun playing this game.

TK gave me a pretty long leash when it came to fun. I have to admit there was a time or two he told me to tone it down. But there were other times, like when I was slumping at the plate, when he told me I need to have more fun, and not get so down.

Mr. Turkey

Pat Reusse is a veteran columnist at the Minneapolis *Star Tribune*. He's an old-time baseball writer who worked his way up to column writing. One of his annual traditions is to pick a Turkey of the Year for his Thanksgiving column.

Like I said earlier, my numbers were pretty solid in 1990. But on Thanksgiving morning I opened up the paper to learn that I had received his Turkey of the Year award. You could say I was a little angry. I certainly didn't think I deserved to be the Turkey of the Year. I didn't shoot anyone or rob a bank, did I?

His logic was that we finished in last place, and that we let it be known that I had turned down more money elsewhere to stay with Minnesota. I guess I shouldn't have said that. And then, yes, I broke my ankle screwing around in the clubhouse, although I think it should be known that we were already about 30 games out of first when that happened.

Reusse and I didn't talk the whole next year, and we never talked a whole lot after that. Other than that, though, I always had a good relationship with the media. There were a lot of stories about my weight, and that got a little old. But it was something to write about, I guess.

I can laugh about being Turkey of the Year now. Every year he runs a list of past winners, and it seems like every Thanksgiving I get a call from someone who says: "I didn't know you were Turkey of the Year."

Yes, I really was. Never the MVP or Rookie of the Year— both of which I felt I could have won—but Turkey of the Year.

That's me.

CHAPTER THIRTEEN

Return to Glory

A New Friend

By the time we reached spring training for the 1991 season, it was a little easier to forget that we had finished last in our division the previous summer. Our front office made a number of significant off-season additions, signing Jack Morris, Chili Davis, and Mike Pagliarulo as free agents, trading for Steve Bedrosian and bringing up a rookie second baseman, Chuck Knoblauch.

Pagliarulo was brought in to replace my old buddy Gary Gaetti, who signed a free agent contract with California during the off-season. Like I said before, Gaetti and I were like brothers early in our careers. But his religious conversion during 1988, and subsequent preaching, changed our relationship. We'd patched things up by the time he left, but I didn't feel like I was missing my brother in spring of '91.

As the '91 season went on, the guy I probably hung around with the most was Knoblauch. It was a little different relationship than I had with Gaetti. I started out the year as Knobby's babysitter more than his buddy.

When he first came up, Knobby was very hot tempered, and could get pretty moody. Our manager, Tom Kelly, essentially gave me the job of babysitting him. Since I played next to him in the field, TK wanted me to make sure that Knobby kept his head in the game. If Knobby struck out at the plate, it was my job to make sure he didn't take it out on the field with him.

When I looked in the dugout, I'd often see TK pointing at me, then pointing at second, and I knew it was time to get Knobby's head on straight. What usually happened is that I'd say something to Knobby, and he'd tell me to go screw myself. So at least I knew he heard me. Some of it must have sunk in.

Knobby had a confident cockiness about him, but he backed it up. He was a rookie, and he knew his role, meaning he knew when he had to move runners up and do all the little things that Kelly demanded. To me, he kind of lost that attitude of being a role guy when he went to the Yankees later in his career. Maybe that's what playing in New York does to a guy. I wouldn't know. Thankfully.

But as the summer of 1991 went on, Knobby became one of those guys you loved to have on your team, but hated to play against. And it wasn't long into the season when I became more of a friend than a babysitter.

Plan in Place

We knew we had a good team when we arrived at spring camp. It was a different feeling than '87. Even though we had some key off-season additions in '87, everything that happened that summer seemed like a surprise. In '91, it was more like we knew we had put together a team that was going to be good. It was a much more planned feeling in '91, and that feeling kind of stuck with us all the way through the year.

The new guys were great, not only on the field but in the clubhouse. I felt like I had an immediate bond with Jack because we were both Minnesota boys. You could feel that. You had to, because Jack was pretty quiet and didn't say a whole lot. But just his presence made a difference. If there's anybody you want on the mound in a big game, it's Jack. I think he had a tremendous impact on our clubhouse, especially our younger pitchers, like Scott Erickson.

Chili Davis is one of the nicest guys I've ever met in the game. I didn't know a thing about him until we signed him, and he just fit in with our crew. He didn't come in wearing a halo like he was here to help save us. He came in with the attitude that he was trying to fit in, and laughed and joked with the rest of us.

It was almost like the front office was looking for guys like that, because Pags was the same way. He came from New York, so he had that Yankee mystique. But he played hard, worked hard, sweated hard and best of all hated the guys on the other team. Pags was a real competitor, and I liked that.

Different Feeling

It wasn't the same kind of closeness that we had on the '87 team. I don't think anything could replace what we had that year, because so many of us had broken into the big leagues together and grown up together. The '91 team was a lot better than the '87 team. In '87, we were more raw, more guts, more bloody—a go-get-em type of lunch box group of players, a bunch of misfits who grew up together.

In '91 we had more talent, and I always had that feeling that we had been put together to win. I just didn't think that team should lose. I know I'd have been more upset if we hadn't won it in '91 than I would have been in '87, because we just plain had a better team.

Here's a trivia question: How many guys were on the World Series roster in both '87 and '91?

The answer: Seven—Kirby Puckett, Dan Gladden, Greg Gagne, Randy Bush, Gene Larkin, Al Newman, and me.

Up and Down

Winning the division didn't come easy for us. And almost nothing came easy for me. We were under .500 in late May, and I was hitting under .250, which was about 50 points higher than I was hitting in mid-May. How bad was I at the start of the season? In mid-April, TK sent Al Newman up to pinch hit for me in the top of the ninth inning.

Newmie was a valuable backup infielder, but he's never going to be known for his bat. In eight big-league seasons, he hit one homer. But he was a switch-hitter, which at the time meant TK thought he had a better chance of getting on base against a left-handed pitcher than me batting left-handed.

The truth is, TK apparently had those thoughts quite a bit by then. By that point, TK had gone to platoon time, which meant I wasn't playing all that much against left-handed pitchers. To this day I think he started platooning too much. He had a reputation as a manager for using his whole bench, and that's fine and good. But you can overdo it.

The first part of my career when I walked into the clubhouse I never even looked at the lineup card. I was hitting cleanup, or maybe fifth against certain left-handers, and playing first base. But then it got to the point where I had to check the lineup card to see if I was playing. It seemed like the last few years I played, I never got into a stretch where I was getting a couple weeks of straight playing time. That's one of the reasons I got tired of playing. It's a huge mind-set change.

It almost got to the point that if we were going against a left-handed pitcher, I assumed I wouldn't be in the lineup. If we saw 10 lefties a month, I probably started against three of them. It wasn't like TK ever sat down with me and told me the reason why. That wasn't his style.

I respected the fact that it's the manager's job to determine who plays. But it pissed me off. I'd be driving to the park not knowing whether I was going to be playing or not. There were days I'd look at the card, see my name in the lineup and be surprised and have to quick get in the frame of mind that I was playing. Baseball's all about routine, and I started getting out of the routine.

Plus, I took some crap about being pinch hit for by Al Newman.

Difference Maker

It's fair to say I probably didn't make a good first impression on our new hitting coach, Terry Crowley. I ultimately turned things around and had a decent season (.284, 20 homers, 89 RBIs), and my power numbers would have been better had it not been for a variety of injuries.

Crow deserves a special mention, not so much for what he did for me, but for the effect he had on several guys. I wasn't a guy who spent a lot of time with hitting coaches or studying pitchers or watching video. I always had the attitude "Full mind, empty bat, empty mind, full bat."

The worst thing about my slump was the advice that came from so many different people. The two people who probably helped me most over the years were Rick Stelmaszek, because he had seen me for so many years, and my mom. There were several times my mom would suggest something, I'd try it and it worked.

I was always changing stances. I'd use one for as long as it felt comfortable, then switch to something else. I've got a huge poster in my "Twins room" at home, and my elbow is way up. I remember exactly when that picture was taken, because it was right after my mom told me to keep my elbow up. I tried it, and it worked for a while. When it stopped working, I dropped my elbow.

I know Crow helped a bunch of guys, and I had a lot of respect for how hard he worked. He was down in what we called "The Hole"—a batting cage under the Dome stands—with players every day, working on swings. Mike Pagliarulo and Randy Bush were always down in The Hole with Crow.

I think it's fair to say that Crow was the best hitting coach we had. I hate saying that, because the guy he succeeded was Tony Oliva. I just think it was difficult for Tony to teach guys how to hit, because he was such a natural.

One time in Seattle, John Moses asked Tony how to hit the pitcher we were facing. Tony looked out at the pitcher, then turned to John and said, "I don't know. I never faced him before." And he was serious. Put a bat in Tony's hand and even then he'd have walked up to the plate and hit the guy. But he had a hard time explaining why or how to players.

Tony's standard line was: "See the ball. Hit the ball." It worked for him. Crow was a little more in-depth with his approach. He was the first hitting coach we had who really worked with the team on hitting. And as the summer went on, Crow's work paid dividends.

Picking Up

There was never any panic about our slow start. There seemed to be a confidence about that club, where we knew we were good and it was only a matter of time. The time came when the calendar flipped over to a new month. On June 1, we started a 15-game winning streak.

I honestly don't remember a whole lot about the streak itself, other than I started hitting better and Scott Erickson basically won every time he started a game. Scotty was another one of the young guys, picked in the same 1989 amateur draft as Knoblauch. Scotty joined the club midway through the 1990 season and made an immediate impact.

In '91 he had one of the most dominating stretches I've ever seen (11-0 from April 25 though June 24). He won 20 games for us in '91, despite battling arm problems from before the All-Star break on. The guy had a nasty, nasty sinkerball. I didn't even want

break on. The guy had a nasty, nasty sinkerball. I didn't even want to play catch with him because of the stuff he had.

We called him Superman, because he looked like Superman—a big, good-looking guy. He was quiet, but he had a little edge to him. In that respect he was a little bit like Knoblauch.

I do remember that our streak reached 15 by sweeping a three-game series at Cleveland. Baseball players are by and large pretty superstitious, and by the time we reached Cleveland that's how our club was. We sat around and drank beer from a keg in the clubhouse after the first game, and because we didn't want to change anything we did it after each game of the series.

That kind of thinking was pretty common in our clubhouse. When we started winning home games in the 1987 postseason, Tom Kelly, who was very superstitious, kept the same home jersey on every day. TK chewed tobacco at the time, and he had stains all over the front of it, and the jersey just plain stunk. But I guess he figured that was a small price to pay for a winning streak.

Of course, when it came to what to do in Cleveland, our options were rather limited. Bill Sheridan, the visiting clubhouse guy in Cleveland, was one of the nicest guys in the league. But he didn't have much to work with. Cleveland had the worst clubhouse in the league, and the worst spreads. Some days you'd come in and there'd be doughnuts that looked like they had been around since Babe Ruth played.

Bill's standard fare was a keg of beer and pizza. He always had pizza out. And you could count on the keg being tapped, because Bill always did that early, so he could get some for himself.

Don't get me wrong: Beer and pizza are right up there on the top of my favorites. But it really didn't compare with, say, Sherm Seeker's ribs at the Dome or the buffet meals in the clubhouse in Anaheim.

But I probably have as many memories from the Cleveland clubhouse as any in the big leagues. Long before the winning streak, there was a night where Gary Gaetti, a couple other guys and I were so frustrated by our losing ways that we sat in the Cleveland clubhouse and basically polished off an entire keg of beer by ourselves.

Moving On

After winning our 15th straight game in Cleveland, we packed up and headed to Baltimore. The streak ended in the first game of the series when the Orioles scored three runs in the bottom of the ninth off our closer, Rick Aguilera, to win 6-5. It's kind of amazing to think how close we were to winning 20 straight, because we won our next four games.

By the end of June my average was back up over .280 thanks to a hot stretch (.359 batting average for the month of June), and we were in first place in the AL West. We ended up cruising to the division title.

We had more pitching depth on that team than any I've ever been on. Erickson, Morris, and Kevin Tapani gave us a Big Three (54 combined victories). Plus we had a great bullpen, with Steve Bedrosian, Carl Willis, and Terry Leach as set-up men and Rick Aguilera as our closer.

I can't say the year was quite as smooth for me. It was one of those years where I was always batting injuries and ended up playing only 132 games.

My most prominent injuries that season included: a strained hamstring in early May, a bruised right shoulder diving for a catch in mid-June, a sprained right ankle on July 1, and finally an injured left shoulder in early September after colliding with Mike Pagliarulo chasing a pop-up. At least I didn't get hurt chasing a clubhouse kid around the locker room.

Hey, even a finely tuned machine falls apart once in a while.

Diversion

I took up a new hobby in the early 1990s: horse racing. Tom Kelly always loved the horses and dogs. As a kid he'd trained trotters in New Jersey, and that love of the racing animals just stuck with him. Late in 1990 he talked Jimmy Wiesner, our equipment manager, and me into becoming partners and buying a horse.

We named our little company "Domeboys." The picture on the back of the racing silk was a horse holding a bat in his mouth. It was kind of cute, if I do say so myself.

We bought our first horse, Verbatim's Pride, for $8,000. All three of the wives immediately became attached to the horse and were going out to the stable, petting him and feeding him carrots during the day.

The first race we entered him in was a $16,000 claiming race, which basically meant that anyone who wanted to buy any of the horses entered put in a $16,000 claim and the horse was theirs. Verbatim's Pride finished third or fourth, and right after the finish TK came up and said, "We just got claimed." Of course he had to explain it to us, and as soon as he did all three of the wives started crying. But TK, Wiesy, and I were thinking that this was pretty easy money. We doubled our purchase price in about a week.

So, of course, we bought a couple other horses. And it's fair to say we never again achieved the financial success we did with our first venture. Green Luck never won a race, Lark's Charm had two wins, and our fourth horse, Albell, had a couple wins and was good enough to enter in a race at Santa Anita.

But overall, I'd guess that we lost money after that very first race. I did get an education. I learned that horses need a drug called Lasix when they suffer from nosebleeds. And that they eat a lot. And that they get hurt about as often as I did. And when they're hurt, they don't run, and when they don't run you can't make any money. But they do continue to eat and go to vet appointments.

Sport of kings? I don't think so.

The Domeboys lasted about three years. After that, I was happy to live vicariously through TK's dog kennel at Hudson. He named a bunch of dogs after me: Hrbek's Heidi, Hrbek's Jeanie, Hrbek's Slam, among others.

To this day I still enjoy watching the dogs race. As far as the horses go, it was fun to stroll the backside as an owner and be a part of it for a while.

The Big News

By far the most important thing to happen to me during the 1991 season came on an off-day in Seattle in early August. We had been on a long road trip, and flew up from California after a game on August 7. Jeanie had called me in California and said she'd like to meet the team in Seattle, and it was always great to have her join me on the road. She loved Seattle, so I figured she was coming out to eat some seafood, walk the wharf, and shop at Pike's Market.

We made dinner reservations at Cutter's, which looks out over the Sound. Before dinner, she gave me a present, wrapped up in a little box. I opened it up, and inside was a pacifier. I'm not a rocket scientist, but I'm able to put two and two together and get four. I was going to be a daddy.

Wow. That's still all I can say. That gave me everything in life I'd ever dreamed of. I had gotten married, and now we were going to have a family. Plus, I'd already played on a World Series winner for my hometown team. What else was there?

I think that might have been the first time it entered my head that I had three years left on my contract, and maybe I'd finish that up and call it a career. I had other things to do with my life.

Jeanie and Heidi visit me on the field at the Dome. Being away from them during the season was difficult, to say the least.
Courtesy of the Minnesota Twins

The Celebration

After our hot stretch in June, we just steadily pulled away. We had an eight-game lead on September 1, and when we clinched the pennant we still had an eight-game lead over the White Sox with seven games left to play.

The day we clinched the pennant was about as nontraditional as you can get. We entered the day with a magic number of one, but lost at Toronto 2-1 in the final game of a three-game series. We didn't know what the White Sox were doing when we climbed onto two team busses and headed to

Hamilton to catch our charter flight. Fortunately, I was on the bus with our manager, Tom Kelly.

Thanks to this new modern technology—the cell phone— our traveling secretary, Remzi Kiratli, and Kelly were able to listen to the final outs of the White Sox' 2-1 loss to Seattle. We couldn't hear the cell phone, of course, but we knew what had happened when TK stood up in the aisle and yelled: "Boys, boys, congratulations. You're the champions of the Western Division." With that, we became the first team in modern time to go from last to first in a single season.

How many major leaguers have clinched a title on a bus? The guys on the second bus heard the news on a delayed basis when their driver received a call from his dispatcher, who had received a call from the driver of our bus. Funny to think about that now, because not everybody was carrying a cell phone back then.

The second bus pulled alongside ours on the Ontario freeway, and we looked out the windows at each other and gave thumbs-up signs. Inside our bus we exchanged hugs and high-fives, and then returned to our seats for the rest of the 30-minute drive to the Hamilton airport. It was pretty subdued, compared to the rowdy celebration we had in the Texas clubhouse after winning the division in '87. We didn't get to celebrate as a team until we all got off our busses at the airport. And that amounted to about 10 minutes of backslapping.

But we didn't get cheated. We flew from Hamilton to Chicago for the start of a series against the White Sox, and when we got to the hotel Remzi told us we had a party room reserved. I'm not going to name the hotel, because we did some damage. We were grown men playing a little boys' game, and that night we let the little boys out.

A lot of it was pretty juvenile stuff, looking back. But it had been a long summer, and the chances to celebrate in this game come few and far between. I remember we broke some tables, jumping up on them, and wrestling. I don't know who did it, but someone had a pair of scissors that ended up in Bedrosian's hands, and he started snipping people's ties off.

That wasn't enough for him, and pretty soon he was sneaking up behind people cutting their sport coats up the back. Chili's clothes got cut up real good that night, and his ride up the elevator became something of a legend. A couple people sharing the elevator looked at him—a black guy with his clothes all cut up—and got scared, thinking he was a bum off the street. What they didn't know was that Chili was a major-league ballplayer, and one of the nicest guys you'd ever meet.

The Postseason

If you're a baseball fan you know the highlights of our 1991 postseason. After beating Toronto in the ALCS, we played in what most people still say is one of the greatest World Series ever, beating Atlanta in seven games. It's a Series remembered for Kirby Puckett's 11th-inning home run in Game 6 to give us a 4-3 victory and Jack Morris' 10-inning shutout for a 1-0 Game 7 victory.

There's not a lot I can add to what's already been said about those exploits. When Puck passed away in the spring of 2006, the Minneapolis *Star Tribune* did a huge story about his performance in Game 6, calling it one of the greatest ever. In addition to the home run, he made a leaping catch to rob Ron Gant of at least an extra-base hit in the third inning. We rode Puck into Game 7, and then turned it over to Jack, which is a pretty good guy to hand it to.

When we came into the clubhouse after Game 6, Jack had Marvin Gaye's "Let's Get It On" playing on the speakers. It was pretty fitting, because that's the way we all felt.

Game 7

The biggest contribution I made in Game 7 came in the top of the eighth when the Braves loaded the bases with one out. Atlanta actually would have had a 1-0 lead had it not been for Greg Gagne successfully playing one of the oldest tricks in the game on Lonnie Smith, who had led off with a single. Terry Pendleton hit a ball into the left-field corner, but Smith for some reason had his eyes on Gagne, who faked as if he was catching a grounder and getting ready to start a double play.

Smith slowed down, and by the time he realized what had happened he only made it to third. After Ron Gant hit a grounder to me for an unassisted out, David Justice was walked intentionally. That brought up Sid Bream, who hit a grounder to me that started a first-to-catcher-to-first double play to end the inning. To this day I can still see Brian Harper catching the ball and throwing it back to me. When I got that ball I gave a hard fist pump, because it was a key play, keeping the game tied 0-0.

That's one of those plays you practice a ton every spring. I'll bet in my whole career, 14 years, I probably made that play three times where we actually got the double play. Most times you get the out at home and don't even make the throw to first.

The next year in spring training when we were doing infield drills TK said, "C'mon, give me the pump Hrbie." Then he hit the ball to me, I threw home to Harp and Harp threw it back to me. I gave the arm pump, and TK said, "We're done for the day."

All Jack Needed

Jack Morris took care of the rest, holding the Braves scoreless until we were finally able to push across a run in the bottom of the 10th. To me, there's no other pitching performance in the history of the World Series that comes close to what Jack did that night. And that includes Don Larsen's no-hit game in 1956.

Jack was so fired up, it was almost like he had an aura around him. He was in such a zone, you could probably have hit him on the head with a sledgehammer and he would have never felt it. It was amazing to see a guy that pumped up, but able to stay in such complete control of those emotions. When Jack needed to make a pitch to get out of a jam, he made the pitch, like he did getting Bream to hit the grounder to me with the bases loaded in the eighth inning.

Watching him pitch that night, it was almost like the rest of us should just have taken a seat and watched him. It was like an out-of-body experience for me, to stand in the field and watch what the guy was doing.

When Jack came in after the ninth inning with the game still scoreless, TK went to him to see how he was feeling. I didn't hear the exchange, but I'm told Jack didn't hesitate, telling TK that he wasn't going to come out, and that it was his game to win or lose. And TK let Jack go out for the 10th inning.

That's the way TK was with pitchers. He wanted to hear what people had to say. If Jack would have wavered, and said something like, "I don't know, I feel pretty good, I think I can go another inning," he'd have been out. But Jack wanted the ball, and that's all TK wanted to hear.

One more inning was all Jack needed to give us. Danny Gladden made a great base-running play to lead off the inning, getting a double on what looked like a bloop single. Knoblauch sacrificed him to third and they walked Puck and me to load the bases with one out. Gene Larkin then etched himself into Minnesota sports history with a long single over a drawn in outfield to give us our second World Series in five years.

I made headlines during the Series, too, although it wasn't something I tried to do, or felt I even deserved. But folks are always going to remember my grand slam in the '87 Series, and Ron Gant and Kent Hrbek in '91.

The Play

I'll be honest with you: I still try to avoid connecting flights through the Atlanta airport because of what happened in Game 2. Harmon Killebrew's son lives in Atlanta, and he says they still hate me down there. They've probably got my picture on a wall next to General Sherman, who burned his way through the city after the Civil War. I can tell you they don't forget the people they think did them wrong.

We had won Game 1 behind Morris 5-2, so Atlanta was desperate not to fall behind two games. Here's the scene: We were up 2-1 in the top of the third of Game 2, and the Braves had Lonnie Smith on first with two out. Gant, the next batter, singled to left, and Danny Gladden made a great play getting the ball to the infield.

What took place next should never have happened, because with a runner on third our pitcher, Kevin Tapani, should have been backing up the catcher behind home plate. But Tap, for some reason, was standing between the pitcher's mound and home plate. Gant was probably more surprised to see Tap in that spot than anyone, because he took a big turn at first, thinking the throw might go home and he'd head to second. But Tap cut the relay off, and I hollered at him to throw to first, which he did.

Gant stopped in his tracks, turned and raced back to first. If he would have slid, he would have been safe. Instead, he came back in trying to stand up. He tried to put one foot on the base and stop himself, but I knew his momentum was going to make him overrun the base. I caught the ball, tagged his leg, and just kept my glove on his leg. I could feel him falling as he tried to stop. I could feel him pushing me backward, and the whole time I just kept my glove on his leg in case he went off the base. And that's exactly what happened. I actually bruised my thigh on the play, because he hit me with his leg as he started to fall backward.

Now, if you watch the play in regular speed, the angle they showed it makes it look like I picked his leg up. Everyone

This play with Atlanta's Ron Gant in Game 2 of the World Series made headlines when Braves fans thought I pushed him off the bag.
Courtesy of the Minnesota Twins

thought that, except the most important person: umpire Drew Coble. I tell everyone who will listen to watch the play in slow motion. You'll see that Gant was falling backward, pushing me back. I did not pick up his leg. I knew he was going to come off the base. That's why I kept my glove on him and held my ground.

The only thing I did wrong was probably have a little too much fun with it after the game. That was during my Baron Von Raschke stage—a professional wrestler known for his Claw hold—when I was talking about a second career as a wrestler after I retired. So naturally the media had some fun talking about my fondness for wrestling, and I joined in the fun. In fact, I said something to the effect that if you ain't cheating, you ain't trying, which might have been the dumbest thing I ever said after a game, because the folks in Atlanta took it as a confession.

It didn't help the mood in Atlanta that we won the game 3-2.

The Reception

It didn't take long for the calls to start coming. My mom got a call at home before she left for Atlanta, telling her that her son better watch out when he got to Atlanta. There were some death threats made, and when I got to the ballpark for Game 3 I had FBI agents waiting to talk to me. They filled me in on the death threats, and said they were taking them seriously.

When we went out to the outfield to stretch before the game, I looked around and I didn't have a teammate close to me. I looked up, saw all the empty space around me and someone yelled, "If they start shooting, we don't want to be anywhere near you." That was cute, but honestly it was pretty serious stuff.

Jeanie was about five months pregnant at the time, and made the trip with me to Atlanta. We had to take the phone off the hook and didn't leave the hotel. Atlanta might be a real nice city, but I wouldn't know. I never saw any of it, because we didn't dare leave the room.

When they introduced me before Game 3, they booed. Every time I came to the plate, they booed. It was definitely an uneasy, unnerving feeling. I had a rough time at the plate in Atlanta, going 1-for-13 in the three games. Personally, I think I just stunk. But subconsciously could the death threats have bothered me? I'm not going to lie—it was a rough time, and there wasn't anything funny about it.

The Aftermath

What always bothered me, to this day, is that Ron Gant never had the balls to come out and say, "I lost my balance. You made a good play." That's always bothered me.

I've never even talked to the guy. I've signed a couple baseballs for fans that had his name on it. I guess people thought it was neat to have both our names on the same ball, although I'm not too fond of being linked with him.

Maybe if they'd have shot me, he'd have come out and said, "Oh, he shouldn't have been shot. I made a base-running blunder." But I've never crossed paths with the guy, which is probably just as well.

But the memory lives on. To this day, that play is the most-asked question I get. I don't care if I'm doing a golf fundraiser, or hunting or fishing. Someone will say, "I always wanted to ask you…" And I'll stop them, and say, "No, I didn't pull him off the base."

It was kind of strange timing, but we had a trip scheduled to the Bahamas in January of 1992, and it had a connection in Atlanta. That seriously was as nervous as I've ever been, anyplace. It felt spooky. I sure didn't have my chest out, saying, "Hey, we just kicked your ass in the Series." It was more like I had my coat over my head, and I just wanted to get on the next flight.

To this day, Atlanta is one city I don't want to visit. I'm pretty sure the *Kent Hrbek Outdoors* TV show wouldn't do very well down there.

In front of our home crowd at the Dome, I thanked the fans on behalf of my teammates for their support. It was special, but didn't feel quite like the 1987 celebration. Courtesy of the Minnesota Twins

The Celebration

That planned feeling about the team that I said we had entering the season stuck with us right to the end. I'm not saying that was bad, it was just different than '87.

I can't even remember how we celebrated after winning Game 7. Maybe that means it was really good. Or maybe it means I just went home and slept. I don't know.

Even the parade was more planned. In '87 they had us in convertibles, and the cars could barely get through the crowd. People reached out and touched us. In '91, we rode in trucks, so we could be above the crowd a little bit.

The '91 team was a better club, but the feeling in the city was a little different. We'd been through it once. I always say it's kind of like having two kids, and people ask which one is more special. Well, they're both special. But there's a feeling the first time you go through something that sticks with you.

One thing that didn't change: I rode in the '91 parade in the same vehicle with Jim Wiesner, our equipment manager.

CHAPTER FOURTEEN

Winding Down

I'll always remember the 1992 season as the first time I seriously began thinking about retirement. It wasn't a passing thought, like when Jeanie told me I was going to be a father the previous summer. The thoughts became a little more intense, a little more real, in '92.

Life changed for me in a lot of ways that summer. Physically, by then, I was hurting all the time. I had dislocated my left shoulder in 1989 and missed six weeks. I dislocated the same shoulder again in spring training of '92.

It wasn't only my shoulders. My knees ached, my ankles ached, my wrists ached. My whole body hurt most days. I took four Tylenol before batting practice, then four more before the game.

My outlook on life changed, too. Our daughter, Heidi, was born during spring training. She had some complications after the birth, and required stomach surgery. I was able to hang around for a couple days, but then I had to get back to training camp to get ready for the season. When I got back to camp, it felt like I'd seen my wife and child for two seconds, then I was out the door.

I was never a big fan of conditioning or stretching and my weight was always a hot topic for the media. Courtesy of the Minnesota Twins

It was three weeks before I could see them again. Every day I'd take batting practice, then run in to call home. Then I'd play the game, and run in to call home. My whole world depended on how those phone calls went. Was Heidi doing well that day? Or was it a bad day?

I guess everything just came to a head in '92. We had a good team, winning 90 games, but it wasn't a championship team. Jack Morris, our big pitching horse, signed a free agent contract with Toronto after '91, and Danny Gladden, who had been our left fielder for two World Series championship teams, signed a free agent deal with the Tigers.

Then, to top it off, I injured my right shoulder in a collision at home plate in late August. I had career lows in homers and RBIs. But it wasn't the numbers as much as the way I felt inside. It got to the point that it wasn't fun anymore.

I'd be at home and look at the clock and say, "Oh, I've got to go to the park today." Before, it was always, "Oh, I get to go to the park today." It wasn't the guys on the team or anything like that. It was just changes with me.

Advice from the Top

My weight had always been a topic of conversation, a lot of it humorous. I came to spring training camp in 1984 and one of my teammates had painted my number, 14, on a Shamu the Whale billboard for Sea World at our ballpark in Orlando. Funny stuff. I laughed at it, too, right along with my teammates. I learned it had been Mark Portugal who painted the number on, and I got even. I can't remember how, but I'm sure I did. I always did.

I was a skinny kid when I came to the majors, but let's just say I grew. And after a while, the jokes weren't as funny to some people. I was playing at about 260 pounds by the '90s, and I knew that Twins officials were thinking that my weight was taking a toll on my knees and ankles, and was probably going to cut my career short.

My manager, Tom Kelly called me in for a heart-to-heart about my weight after the 1992 season. TK laid everything on the table, and I pretty much told him that this was me. I didn't totally neglect my conditioning. I had tried, at various times, to watch my weight and work out in the off-season. But I was never going to be a fanatic about it. I told him I wasn't trying to shortchange anyone, but this is what you're getting.

TK told a reporter after I retired that he felt terrible walking out of that meeting, and decided he'd never have that talk with me again. I gave everything I had on the field. I played hurt, I dived for balls, I took the extra base. And TK knew that better than anyone.

I always said if they had someone who could take my job away from me, then he could have it. But that never happened.

Wanting to spend more time with my daughter, Heidi, was one of the main reasons I decided to call it quits in 1994. Courtesy of the Minnesota Twins

Full Circle

Nothing happened the next two summers to change my thinking about retirement. My batting average was declining, and the team hit the skids. We had losing seasons in both '93 and '94, and it became increasingly clear to me that I would finish out the five-year deal I signed after the 1989 season, and retire at the end of '94.

I was 34 when I walked away. I could still hit the ball, and I'm sure I could have hung on and played a few more years. But that wasn't the way I wanted to go out, hanging on to make a few more bucks. I wanted to walk away while I still could, while I was still having some fun.

Yes, we had losing seasons my final two years. But I felt lucky, because my manager was still Tom Kelly, and the coaching staff, including my old minor-league manager Rick Stelmaszek, was still pretty much intact. That made those final years special. And it meant a lot to me to play my whole career with the Twins. I didn't want to lose that.

As much as anything, I had this thing about retiring, probably because my dad died when he was 52 and never got to retire. To me, retiring was a good thing. It meant you could go off and do whatever you wanted.

That's bad?

The Announcement

I didn't make any attempt to keep it a secret that 1994 was going to be my last season. If reporters asked about retiring, I told them the truth. I finally made it official with a press conference the first week in August. We had to do it then, because baseball was heading toward a strike that would end the season on August 10.

The strike didn't have anything to do with my decision. I certainly felt bad about the strike, and what it did to the game by

I announced my retirement from baseball at a press conference. I have no regrets about leaving when I did. Does this guy look sad?
Courtesy of the Minnesota Twins

knocking out the World Series. But I was going to retire after the 1994 season no matter what. It just came a couple weeks earlier than I'd have liked.

It wasn't a real emotional press conference, except for the part where I talked about my dad never getting to retire. As far as I was concerned, this was a joyful time. I had a little kid growing up, and I was going to be able to spend time with my family. I was ready to move on and try something new. It wasn't like I was being forced out. That would have been tough, I think. But I was walking away on my own terms.

It's almost fitting that two days before what was going to be my final game, I sprained my ankle. But TK told me that if I could walk, he wanted me to be on the field. He said I'd meant too much to the organization to go out sitting on the bench.

So I played. Big deal. I'd been playing hurt for the last few years. I got standing ovations every time I came to the plate my final game. And I caught the pop-up that ended the game. I always thought that was a neat way to have it end.

Looking Back

Some things never changed during my career. There was always someone saying that I had "Hall of Fame" talent, and asking what might have been had I devoted myself to physical conditioning.

When I retired, naturally someone asked Tom Kelly if I had Hall of Fame talent. "I sure think so," he said. My teammate, Gene Larkin, said some nice things, then added: "I just wish he had stayed in better shape, from a fan's point of view. But that's him."

Geno's still a close friend, by the way. The thing is, I understand all those comments. I just hope people understand me when I say I couldn't be happier the way my career turned out. The day I popped out of my mom's belly I had a gift that allowed me to hit a baseball. It just came natural. To me, that was something to be proud of, not feel bad about.

I was proud that I played the game hard, and competed. I was proud that we played the game the right way, and represented Minnesota well on and off the field. My shoulders were the first part of my body to go, and that was because I dived for balls on the hard turf of the Dome. It didn't have anything to do with weight.

Sure, I wish I could have been in better shape. But that just wasn't me. I was a throwback in a lot of ways, and I guess that was one of them. I'd have been a lot more at home having a beer and hot dog with Babe Ruth than working out at some gym with modern ballplayers who want to look like body builders.

Hall of Fame talent? Harmon Killebrew is a Hall of Famer, and I see him every once in a while at charity events and Twins functions. Harmon is a great guy, but does being a Hall of Famer make him any different than me? He gets more money for his autograph than I do, but otherwise we're not that different, as far as I can see. And what about guys like Bert Blyleven and Tony Oliva? If I had a vote, they'd both be in the Hall of Fame. But are they any different now than they would be if they were in the Hall of Fame?

And here's the thing to remember with some Hall of Famers: Ted Williams never won a World Series. Harmon never won a Series. Ernie Banks never won a Series. A lot of guys who have plaques in Cooperstown never won a Series.

I was fortunate enough to be a part of two Series champions. And that, to me, was the ultimate. It was the reason I played this game. If I was a tennis player, I'd have felt different, because that's all individual. But baseball to me was a team game. You lived and breathed baseball every day from February through October with your teammates and coaches. You won together, you lost together.

To have your name on a championship trophy, that's the only plaque that really mattered to me. And to win those championships in a small market like Minnesota—and in my hometown city—that makes it even more special. I walk around here today and people still smile, because when they see me they remember 1987 and 1991. That's what I played for.

Awards

If I'm not obsessed with the Hall of Fame you can probably guess that I'm not overly concerned with individual awards. I can take them or leave them, although I would have liked to have taken a couple more during my career—namely a Gold Glove. That's one thing that always eats at me. I took a great deal of pride in my defense, and I know if you talk to my manager and teammates, they'll say I was a great first baseman who saved a lot of runs with my glove.

I honestly thought I should have won five or six of them. I took a lot of pride in catching the baseball, and I didn't think there was anybody better than I was at first base. To this day, I still feel that there wasn't anybody better at first base.

One of the best compliments I ever got from an opponent came from Dwight Evans, after he singled and was standing at first base with me. A lot of times those days they were sticking left fielders or third basemen at first base to get another bat in the lineup. I'd been a first baseman since ninth grade. Dwight said to me: "Hrbie, they can stick anybody at first base, but nobody can play it like you can."

The truth is I've got one Gold Glove in my basement. Gary Gaetti won four straight Gold Gloves with the Twins (1986-89), and he gave me one of his. He told me that if I wouldn't have caught all the shit he threw over to first base, he'd have never won one.

That's pretty special, coming from a teammate.

And as long as we're talking individual awards, I'll admit it: I thought I should have won the Rookie of the Year in 1982. You look at the numbers, and I had a better year than Cal Ripken

(.301 average, .363 on-base percentage, 23 homers, 92 RBIs to Ripken's .264 average, .317 on-base percentage, 28 homers, 93 RBIs). And in '84, when I was second to Willie Hernandez, a reliever, well, all I can say is that he had a great year, but there area lot of people who believe pitchers shouldn't be MVP. They've got their own award: the Cy Young.

But I can live with that. I'll ride off into the sunset with the two World Series.

The Biggest Honor

The Twins had a special day for me at the Dome in 1995. Before the game, they had a ceremony announcing that the team was retiring my number. My jersey, 14, is up on the outfield wall with Harmon Killebrew, Tony Oliva, Rod Carew and Kirby Puckett. We're the only five Twins who have ever had their number retired.

That's probably the greatest personal honor I've ever had in my life. It's an incredible feeling for me to walk into the Dome and see my number hanging there. And then you think about the other people whose numbers are out there with me. I know I've said this before, but I still think of this when I walk into the Dome: I used to be Tony-O playing wiffle ball in my backyard. And now my number is hanging next to his on the outfield wall. Who'd have thunk?

If I go to a Twins game now with some buddies, and their kids, or maybe their nephews and nieces, it's fun to think that one day those kids will be telling their friends that they met the guy who once wore No. 14. It's pretty awesome to think that when I'm 95 and walk into the Twins stadium, my number is going to be hanging on the wall.

The other thing that happened during the ceremony was just as special: My Twins teammates gave me a trophy for being a good teammate. That's all I ever wanted to be: a good teammate to the guys I played with.

The night was a little emotional. But it's hard to be emotional when you see your buddies and start talking about baseball, and sharing stories. Pretty soon, it was just a party, back with my teammates, having fun, sharing all those old memories. There's not a bad memory in the group—even the one where I busted my ankle chasing a kid around the clubhouse. It might not be the greatest memory, but it's pretty funny and pretty stupid that I'd do something like that.

Heck, without that I might not have been Turkey of the Year.

CHAPTER FIFTEEN

Where's It Heading?

Sometimes I wonder if the Twins will ever have another Kent Hrbek. Or whether anyone will. I'm not talking talent. I'm talking about a guy who grows up idolizing a ballplayer who played his whole career with his favorite team, and then became that ball player. That was me as a kid looking up to Tony Oliva. Both of us Twins for life.

When I think about the future of baseball, loyalty is the first thing that comes to mind. I know steroids and Barry Bonds and Mark McGwire's Hall of Fame vote have dominated the headlines, but I think the biggest problem the game faces is loyalty, and that's obviously linked to the huge amounts of money they throw at players.

You just don't see guys playing their whole careers with one team anymore. If there's one thing I'd like to see in the game, it's that the guys have a little more allegiance to their team, a little more loyalty. I wish guys would get to know more about the city they're playing in.

One of the things that made the Twins special in the '80s was that a lot of the guys bought homes here and made the city their home. Guys like Kirby Puckett and Gary Gaetti became part of the community. When you win a World Series and you're part of the community, it's a whole different level of feeling and meaning.

I understand why it's difficult to be loyal to your franchise. If teams are going to throw huge amounts of money at players, what are you going to do? The game's a little out of whack right now.

I don't want to pick on anyone, but take a guy like Gary Matthews. Before 2006 he was a career .250 hitter who had never even hit 20 homers. He played with a Texas team in 2006 where he was surrounded by some other guys who could hit. And Matthews hit over .300 with 19 homers, and the Angels signed him for $50 million for five years. I understand why Matthews can't be loyal to Texas, but where are the Angels coming from?

My Team

I'm a big fan of what the Twins have been able to do with a small market payroll. But now that they have some legitimate stars, how are they going to keep their nucleus together when the Angels are paying Gary Matthews $10 million a year?

How are the Twins going to pay Justin Morneau in this marketplace? Or Joe Mauer, Johan Santana and Joe Nathan?

It's a funny game. At the start of 2006 people were wondering whether Michael Cuddyer could play in the big leagues. But he had one good year, and now he's supposedly a superstar.

The game's changed a lot from 1981 when I broke in. That's not that long ago, but it seems like a different era.

TK

I feel fortunate that I was able to play most of my career with Tom Kelly as my manager. TK was a throwback, too. His attitude about the game fit with the way I felt about the game, and I think

My manager, Tom Kelly, proudly holds the 1987 World Series championship trophy. I was fortunate to have played for TK because we shared the same respect for the game. Courtesy of the Minnesota Twins

we had a bond because of that. I can't say we were close off the field, or ever hung out together very much. But I was always comfortable with TK, because I knew the attitude he had about the game.

His ultimate goal was to try to play the game hard, and do the best you can. Pretty simple. But apparently it's not so easy to do, because how many organizations are able to embrace that philosophy?

With TK, no one player was bigger than the game. He didn't want guys who wanted to go out and put on a show. He wanted guys who cared about their teammates, and put winning above everything else.

When Andy MacPhail was our general manager, he said it was sometimes difficult to add talent to our roster because TK put such an emphasis on the kind of people he wanted in his clubhouse. Some guys just wouldn't fit in the Twins clubhouse, and from what I see Ron Gardenhire has retained a lot of that philosophy.

I'll give you an example from when I played: When we were looking for a leadoff hitter, some writers thought Rickey Henderson, who was on the market, would be a perfect fit. I knew there was no way Rickey Henderson could be a Minnesota Twin, and if I ever needed that belief reinforced, it came on a winter trip I took with my wife to the Bahamas.

Putting On a Show

I've never understood ballplayers who have that air about them that they're better than other people. I was fortunate enough to be good at a game that people cared about and enjoyed watching. I never saw it as anything more than that, and I never saw it as something that made me better than anyone else.

Sadly, there are some ballplayers who do. We were walking through the Casino at Paradise Island one winter, and here came Rickey Henderson. He was decked out to the max, with clothes and a gold chain, and he had about 15 people around him. I mean he was walking around like he was King Tut.

I was walking around in shorts and a T-shirt. I looked at him, bobbing around, leading a crowd of people, and I said: "You've got to be kidding." But he had to put on a show wherever he was.

People like that didn't play with the Twins. TK wouldn't have picked up Randy Moss, and he would never have allowed Terrell Owens in his clubhouse. Terrell Owens' whole persona is that he's bigger than the game, bigger than his teammates. When you score a touchdown and you stop to sign your name on a ball, that's not respect for the game. That's a joke. Some little kid is going to try to do that, and that's sad.

Kirby Puckett was one of the greatest players in modern baseball, but he never had an air about him or traveled with an entourage. Puck was just another guy in our clubhouse, and that was one reason our clubhouse was what it was. We didn't have people who had that air about them. We were a bunch of ballplayers who loved playing the game.

I'll tell you a guy TK would have in his clubhouse: Kevin Garnett of the Timberwolves. There's a guy I admire for his loyalty to his team and his community. He just goes out and plays hard every night.

If you're playing tennis, or an individual sport, you can go out and blow up your skirt to try to impress the crowd. But if you're playing a team game, don't go out and try to be bigger than your team.

You Cheat, You're Out

I feel a lot more comfortable talking about loyalty and playing the game right than I do some of the other problems with baseball—steroids, for instance.

Our biggest division rival was the Oakland A's, featuring the Bash Brothers—Jose Canseco and Mark McGwire. They've both been implicated in baseball's steroid scandal, and if it's proven that they used steroids to beat us, I'd be angry. But I never heard anything about steroids, and never even heard anyone talk about them.

Of course we all knew Canseco and McGwire were big guys, but when we visited Oakland, they were always at the ballpark early, lifting weights and working out with their coach, Dave McKay. We'd see those guys walk across the field to lift before the A's would take the field for stretching and batting practice.

Maybe I was just dumb, because I never suspected anything. But then my steroids were a Budweiser after the game. I ate Tylenol before games, and drank Budweiser after. And never once did I suspect anyone else—with the Twins or other teams—was doing anything different.

Stimulants Available

Amphetamines were different. Guys took beans, greenies, amphetamines—whatever you want to call them. I'm told that in the days when Harmon Killebrew and Tony Oliva played, they left them sitting out in the clubhouse and you could just walk over and get them whenever you wanted.

It wasn't quite that open when I played. You knew the guys in the clubhouse who had them, if you wanted them. I'm not going to say who used them and who didn't, but they were around. Just put it that way.

I tried them once. I got so wired and so goofy, I just said to myself that I wasn't going to do that anymore. It was one day, and that was it. I went back to my pregame Tylenol. A cup of coffee was as much stimulant as I could take.

Personal Opinion

I take a fairly tough attitude when it comes to cheating. I guess my views probably go back to Pete Rose and his betting on baseball games. I loved Pete Rose to death, the way he played the game. He got more hits than anybody, and his hit total probably won't ever be caught.

But the guy broke one of the biggest rules written on the walls of every clubhouse: DO NOT BET ON BASEBALL.

Period. Pete Rose broke that rule. It's too bad, but in my view he never belongs in the Hall of Fame because of what he did.

I'm keeping an open mind on the steroid scandal until guilt is actually proven. Right now there's a lot of talk, a lot of speculation, but we really don't have solid proof on a guy like Barry Bonds. You look at him early in his career and he was a little pipsqueak, and now he's a huge guy. But you know what? I was a little pipsqueak when I broke into the big leagues, and all I did to get big was eat and drink beer.

So I'll keep an open mind.

Modern Players

I don't want to make it sound like everything about my era was the good old days. I honestly think the players today are better than we ever were. I know for certain they're in better physical shape, and as athletes they can do more.

That may not extend to pitchers, because you can only throw a ball so hard or make it curve so much. But pitchers today do have one built-in advantage, I think. Before expansion began in the 1960s, hitters would see the same pitchers over and over again, and I think it's easier to hit when you know exactly what the pitcher has. Now, with 32 teams and inter-league play, you don't get to see the same pitchers that often, and that's tougher on the hitters.

I sometimes wonder if I'd even make the ball club if I were playing today. The guys today work out 11 months of the year to stay in shape. I was in shape to do what I needed to do. I could go from first to third, from second to home. But I wasn't a guy who worked out 11 months a year, and I wasn't the kind of athlete most guys are today.

Then again, it was different when I played than it was in the 1950s. People wouldn't have worried about my weight if I had been playing in the '50s. Guys didn't work out year-round back then. In fact, when the season was done, they'd get a job selling cars or something. My first manager, Billy Gardner, went back to Connecticut in the off-season and worked in a meat-cutting plant.

That's the era I broke in on. I'm a lot closer to that era than I am to the modern-day athlete. In that sense, I am a throwback. My weight's a lot closer to the old-time ballplayers, too. What can I say? I'm just a guy who loves to eat, and that's true to this day. I know I need to lose 50 pounds.

My wife tries to make me low-fat meals, but what I do is eat twice as much. So that diet plan doesn't seem to be working. But she hasn't given up on me.

CHAPTER SIXTEEN

Life After Baseball

Joy of Nothingness

I guess a lot of people have some sort of master plan when they retire. Not me. Do you know how many sunsets you see playing in the Metrodome? Well, that was my master plan: To be able to be somewhere where I could watch the sunset. And to spend time with my family.

All right, I'll admit it: Basically, I just wanted to sit around and do nothing whenever I felt like it. I certainly didn't want to be a hanger-on in baseball. I didn't like those guys when I played, because to me they just took up space. Let some kid have a chance. I'm sure if I'd have wanted to keep playing, there would have been some team that would have picked me up and shoved me out there a couple more years.

No way that would have compared to what I experienced in retiring. The first thing I did when I retired was buy a 30-foot camper trailer, and haul it down and park it at a campground at Lake Elysian south of the Twin Cities where my in-laws and friends had been going for years. I'm sure people wondered why we didn't buy a million-dollar home on Gull Lake or some other prestigious area. But that campground was where our family and friends were, and that meant more to us than owning some fancy place.

I just liked the atmosphere of that campground. I walked from fire to fire, drinking beer, telling stories and listening to the Twins on the radio. That's living. I'd been there before, at the end of seasons, and I knew just about everyone in the campground. After I retired we spent a lot of time there, and to this day the camper is still parked there.

The other thing I did the summer I retired was get together with a bunch of my buddies and rent a house boat for a fishing trip on Rainy Lake up by the Canadian border. That was something I'd always wanted to do, but I'd never had a chance because of baseball.

Raising Money

I could keep busy when I wanted to. For the first several years, Jeanie and I were still heading a charity golf tournament for ALS, or Lou Gehrig's disease, something we had started doing while I was still playing. It was basically us, along with three or four others, organizing the event. I made a lot of the phone calls, and spent a lot of time on the computer, because I wanted to be hands-on.

If someone asked who was in cart 3A, I knew who it was. I had been to enough golf tournaments where you ask who was in 3A, and they didn't know they had a 3A. Running the tournament could have been a full-time job, and about three years ago we decided to go a different route.

Doug Mientkiewicz had hosted a fishing tournament, and when he left we took that over. It's a little more up my alley than golf. Between the two of them—golf and fishing—we've raised about $4 million for ALS, which is something we're proud of. It's always been important to me to fight ALS, because it claimed my dad at such a young age.

We're in the process now of starting a Kent and Jeanie Hrbek Foundation. Part of the money will go to ALS, and we're talking about where else we want it to go—maybe something with Bloomington youth athletics. We're trying to keep ourselves involved in the community, because this is home and always will be.

I'm also employed by the Twins as a special assistant, which basically means I lobbied for a new stadium and shook a bunch of hands. Kind of following in the footsteps of Tony Oliva again.

New Venture

About a year after I retired, a friend of mine, Eric Gislason, a TV reporter I had met playing for the Twins, asked if I'd ever thought of doing an outdoor show. I told him it sounded fun, but it also sounded like a lot of work and I just wanted to retire.

It took about eight years for Eric to bring the subject up again. It sounded a little better this time. He had some people lined up interested in doing the camera work, so the basic structure was there. I talked to my wife and she encouraged me to give it a try. The show is *Kent Hrbek Outdoors*, and we've just completed our third year. We film about 17 shows a year, and we're on network TV in most Minnesota markets, plus several others in the Upper Midwest. We've even got a station in Oregon that carries the show.

I've enjoyed it, because it's a different kind of work than going to the ballpark and putting on a jock and spitting tobacco. I'm not a big book learner, but it's given me a chance to learn a few things about the TV industry, and I've found it to be interesting. I've even learned some of the ins and outs of selling, and watched them edit and put the show together. When you're part of a small production company, you learn to be a jack-of-all-trades.

Eric and I plan the shows and set up trips, and I've gotten a lot of the guests lined up through contacts I made playing ball.

Eric Gislason and I started up our outdoor show called *Kent Hrbek Outdoors.* Courtesy of *Kent Hrbek Outdoors*

Over the years we've had Joe Mauer, Bobby Knight, Ron Gardenhire, Minnesota governors Tim Pawlenty and Jesse Ventura, South Dakota governor Mike Rounds, plus several former Vikings like Wally Hilgenberg and Mike Morris.

I also got Torii Hunter, although I don't talk a lot about that one. Torii's the closest we've come to a disaster. He stumbled and almost fell out of a boat fishing in southern Minnesota. That's all I need, to bring Torii into the clubhouse with a broken ankle. I've already been down that road myself as a player.

Highlights

As you might guess, I've had some great experiences filming *Kent Hrbek Outdoors*. I'd have to say the best trip was in the summer of 2005 when we went fishing in Alaska. The fishing was fantastic, but the scenery of the country was about 90 percent of what made it so special.

The most unique trip was to Finland with the Rapala fishing people to tour their home base in Finland. Of course we found time to do some fishing there, too, and it felt a lot like fishing in northern Minnesota.

Mostly, we're looking for good stories to tell. I watched *All-American Sportsman* with Curt Gowdy as a kid, and I loved it. I'm not saying that's what our show is, but we try not to be the typical fishing show. I'm not sitting in a boat telling people how to catch bass, or what bait to use. We're telling stories about the people we're with.

The best stories we've done, to me, involve kids. I thought we had a real good show about a camp in South Dakota for kids who are deaf. The camp is funded by proceeds from pheasant hunters, and it's a great use of the money. It was really fun to see the smiles on the kids' faces at the camp, getting a chance to swim and fish. To me, that's the kind of story we like to tell. Something with an outdoors theme that's heartwarming.

We're always on the lookout for stories that are a little offbeat. I thought one of the cool stories we did was to go ice fishing on Mille Lacs with Eddie Lyback. His mom and dad started renting ice houses for fishing on his end in 1954. All they do is ice fishing, nothing in the summer.

Eddie's mom, Phyllis Lyback, who is now 86, is still up there. She wrote a book a few years ago called *50,000 Holes*—great title for a book about ice fishing. The book is about their experience running the business since moving up from Minneapolis years ago.

You never know where ideas are going to come from. We just did a story that came off an email from a guy named Karry Kyllo in Grand Forks. He said he loved to catch catfish in the Red River and wanted to know if we'd like to come up and give it a try. We had no idea who the guy was. He could have been a serial killer who was going to wrap the anchor around our legs and throw us in. He turned out to be a great guy, and I learned a ton about the Red River and catching catfish.

It's kind of funny now, I'll get more people who come up to me and say they watch *Kent Hrbek Outdoors* than say they remember me as a Twin. I'm sure they remember baseball, but the first thing most people mention is the TV show.

Time Well Spent

I honestly can't say that I've missed baseball. If I've missed it, it's only been a little bit, and that's mostly when the playoffs roll around. That's when I start remembering how special 1987 and 1991 were, not only for our team but for the entire Midwest. But watching sunsets, whether it's in my backyard or fishing on a lake, has been everything I hoped it would be.

Even the first year I retired, I didn't have any feelings that I had made the wrong decision. I went to spring training that first year with Jeanie and Heidi, but I didn't spend a lot of time at the ballpark. I did stuff with my family, like regular people do when they go to Florida on a family vacation. We went fishing, sat by the pool and basically did whatever we wanted to.

I don't want to make it sound like a hardship, but baseball is tough on families. From the middle of February until the end of September—and into October if you're lucky—you're never around for family functions. You miss family weddings, birthdays, graduations, and just regular get-togethers. I'm certainly not saying that ballplayers don't get compensated for it, but I don't think you can put a dollar figure on basically not being able to be a part of your family for about nine months a year.

Still Around

I'm still a huge Twins fan, and I'll always be proud of what the Minnesota Twins accomplished when I played. I've been a fan of the club since I was a kid, and now I'm a fan again.

I've had people ask me if I'd ever be interested in coaching or teaching kids how to hit, and the answer is no. Coaching would be right back to the travel and the commitments and missing family time and sunsets.

As far as teaching hitting, I think I'd be lousy at it. For as long as I can remember, I could hit. I never really had to work at it. In that sense, I was a lot like Tony Oliva, because it came natural. How do you teach that? I'd probably be better teaching kids how to golf, because that's something I had to work at to become halfway decent.

When it comes to being involved in baseball, I'm perfectly happy being a special assistant for the Twins. When the club wants me to make an appearance or help out, I'm happy to do it. The Twins have been great keeping people like Harmon Killebrew, Rod Carew, Tony Oliva, and me involved with the club. I don't think many other organizations have tried as hard as the Twins to mix their history with the present.

To me, the No. 1 guy—Mr. Twin—is Tony Oliva. He's kept his home in Bloomington all these years, and has always been around the club in some capacity. He's at the ballpark every night, shaking hands and talking with fans. And you can tell by the smiles that he loves it as much as the fans.

Whenever I look at Tony, it reminds me that the game is more than what you see on the field. It's about the friendships and the characters that you meet along the way.

Tony grew up in Cuba, and to this day he still has a hard time with the English language. While I played, Rick Stelmaszek was always writing down Tony-isms, and there were some great ones, many of them involving the telephone, which always was a challenge for Tony's grasp on English.

Tony would call the eight o'clock number, instead of 800. One time in New York, Tony got a call in the clubhouse before the game from someone that Tony had promised to leave tickets for, but had forgotten to do it. Nobody left more tickets than Tony. We could hear Tony on the phone: "Yeah. Yeah. OK. All right. I sorry. OK." And when he hung up the phone he turned around and said, "Who was that?" He forgot to ask the name of the guy who called. So he walked around the clubhouse muttering to himself, "Who was I talking to? Who was that?"

That was classic Tony. What a character.

There are plenty of characters in baseball—enough of them to have kept me laughing for 14 years in the big leagues.

The Future

I can't say I know exactly what my plans are for the future. We talk about a lot of things. Maybe we'll pack up someday and move west. I've always loved the Black Hills area, and I've never spent a lot of times in the mountains further west.

It sounds ideal, except for one thing: I don't know if I could ever leave Minnesota. Our families are here, our friends and our memories. I don't know if I could ever leave all that behind.

And I still love the involvement I have with the Twins, going to the ballpark when I want to and visiting with people. It's exciting to think about a new ballpark opening in 2010, and I want to be a part of that in some way. I'll never get to play there, but there's going to be a couple World Series banners, and my number is going to be hanging on the outfield wall, right alongside Harmon Killebrew, Rod Carew, Kirby Puckett, and Tony Oliva.

Not bad company.

The one thing I know is that my friend and agent, Ron Simon, has made it possible for me to live out my dreams. I always told Ron that when I retire, the two things I want are to be able to go through the McDonald's drive-thru without worrying about paying for my order, and when I'm done eating to be able to get a dozen minnows to go fishing with.

If I can keep doing that the rest of my life, I'll be happy.

Acknowledgments

It's been a great ride, playing in the big leagues for 14 seasons and winning two World Series championships with my hometown team. I owe a lot of people thanks, more than I can even start to name. But here, in keeping with baseball tradition, is a starting nine:

1. Ed and Tina Hrbek, my older brother Kevin and younger sister Kerry: Without my parents, I'd have never made it to the major leagues. They were the ones who encouraged me as a youngster, who brought me to the ballparks, watched my games and took me home afterward. They never pushed me into baseball, but they must have seen that I loved the game and had a gift for playing it. I could have had a terrible time when I learned at age 20 that my dad was going to die of ALS. But my dad told me that summer to stick with baseball, that he had gotten me that far, and it was up to me to take it from there. That allowed me to go on, and I never forgot those words. After my dad died, my mom became my biggest fan and even offered advice from time to time on

hitting. She passed away in 2005 after battling cancer. I used to talk to her almost daily, and to this day I miss her terribly. When I come home from a fishing trip, it just doesn't feel right not giving her a call and telling her about it. I was lucky to have them as parents. I'm lucky to have Kevin and Kerry as my brother and sister, too. They supported me, too, and I've never had the feeling that they were ever jealous of the success I had. I know it can be hard to be a brother and sister of a so-called celebrity, but they never let that change our relationship, and I'll always be thankful to them for that.

2. Jeanie and Heidi Hrbek: They gave me the family I always dreamed of. Between the two of them, they gave me a reason to stay on the straight and narrow. I'm a guy who could have gone down a lot of wrong roads had I been single, living in Minneapolis and playing in the big leagues. But that would have gotten real old real quick, compared to what I have. Jeanie and Heidi have given meaning to everything I've been fortunate enough to accomplish.

3. Gene and Doris Burns: Jeanie's mom and dad became my second parents. They became the people who took care of all the things at home when I was off playing baseball. When Heidi was born and I went off to spring training, they were the ones who stayed with Jeanie, and helped her make it through those first few weeks. Grandparents are the best. Without them, I don't know what the hell we'd do.

4. Buster Radebach: I don't think I could have had a better high school coach at Bloomington Kennedy than Buster. He played minor-league ball in the Red Sox

organization and knew more about the game than anybody I'd ever met. I learned that the game should be fun from him, and to always remember that it's a game. But he also taught me about the little ins and outs of the game that I didn't even know existed—the game within the game. He brought my understanding to a new level, which allowed me to get to the next level of pro ball after leaving Kennedy.

5. Rick Stelmaszek: Yes, I didn't care much for Stelly when I got stuck with him for a manager as a 19-year-old at Wisconsin Rapids. It's hard to like a guy as tough and mean as Stelly was those years. Now I know why he did it: He was trying to make me grow up, to get me to the big leagues. I had Stelly as a coach my whole career with the Twins, and he grew on me. He was a constant for me, a guy who could offer tips on hitting and life. He became a friend as much as a coach.

6. Tom Kelly: TK and I shared the same values for the game. Pretty simple values: Respect the game, respect your teammates, give your best. Any player is lucky when he's able to play for a manager who he can be on the same page with, and that's what I had. Plus, TK was my mom at the ballpark. I told him that several times. Let's just say he knew when I had my hand in the cookie jar, and when he gave me that look, I understood what it meant.

7. Ron Simon: I had so much confidence in Ron as my agent that I never had to worry about the business part of the game. Ron's a native Minnesotan, and he understood how much it meant to me to play for the Twins. But he was crafty enough to make the Twins believe I'd have left if the money wasn't close. And Ron

made certain the Twins were close. He's made it possible for me to eat McDonald's and buy minnows as often as I want, which is all I ever really wanted from the business side of baseball.

8. Twins fans: They're simply the best. No fans have ever come alive the way the Twins fans did in 1987. Will anyone ever forget 50,000-plus fans jammed into the Dome for a welcome home after we won at Detroit in the '87 ALCS? Or the ticker-tape parade? They let me go out and play a game I love, cheering for me, and embracing me. There was a lot of me to embrace, but they did it.

9. The Twins organization: I'm not even going to try to name a single person in the organization, because there are too many who have been so good to me over the years. The Twins gave me a chance as a 21-year-old kid to make the jump from Class A to the big leagues. I think they gave me that shot a little quicker because things weren't going so well in 1981, and I was a kid from Minnesota who they thought they'd take a gamble on. No one ever told me that, but I've always thought that. I probably surprised them with that homer in my first game. I never saw the minors again, and I never played in any other big-league uniform. Some people might think it's corny when I say it, but that means a lot to me. I can't thank the Twins enough for all they've done for me. The organization remains a part of my everyday life today.

I guess all those wiffle ball games in the backyards of Bloomington paid off.

What a ride.

Anyone for McDonald's and a little fishing?

Index

183